Coastal Change from Hurricane Sandy and the 2012–13 Winter Storm Season: Fire Island, New York

By Cheryl J. Hapke, Owen Brenner, Rachel Hehre, and B.J. Reynolds

Open-File Report 2013–1231

U.S. Department of the Interior
U.S. Geological Survey

U.S. Department of the Interior

SALLY JEWELL, Secretary

U.S. Geological Survey

Suzette M. Kimball, Acting Director

U.S. Geological Survey, Reston, Virginia: 2013

For more information on the USGS—the Federal source for science about the Earth, its natural and living resources, natural hazards, and the environment—visit *http://www.usgs.gov* or call 1–888–ASK–USGS

For an overview of USGS information products, including maps, imagery, and publications, visit *http://www.usgs.gov/pubprod*

To order this and other USGS information products, visit *http://store.usgs.gov*

Suggested citation:
Hapke, C.J., Brenner, Owen, Hehre, Rachel, and Reynolds, B.J., 2013, Coastal change from Hurricane Sandy and the 2012–13 winter storm season—Fire Island, New York: U.S. Geological Survey Open-File Report 2013-1231, 37 p.

Contents

Figures

Tables

Conversion Factors

SI to Inch/Pound

Multiply	By	To obtain
Length		
meter (m)	3.281	foot (ft)
kilometer (km)	0.6214	mile (mi)
kilometer (km)	0.5400	mile, nautical (nmi)
meter (m)	1.094	yard (yd)
Volume		
cubic meter (m^3)	35.31	cubic foot (ft^3)
cubic meter (m^3)	1.308	cubic yard (yd^3)
cubic meter (m^3)	0.0008107	acre-foot (acre-ft)

Vertical coordinate information is referenced to the North American Vertical Datum of 1988 (NAVD 88).

Horizontal coordinate information is referenced to the North American Datum of 1983 (NAD 83).

Elevation, as used in this report, refers to distance above the vertical datum.

Acknowledgments: We are truly indebted to the efforts and assistance from our National Park Service partners, especially Jordan Raphael, Patti Rafferty, Michael Bilecki, and Chris Soller.

We thank Barry Irwin and Phil Thompson of the U.S. Geological Survey (USGS) for providing valuable field assistance. Amy Farris (USGS) contributed to this effort by creating code and deriving the mean high water shorelines from field data. Betsy Boynton (USGS) provided considerable assistance with layout and formatting of the report. We also thank Erika Lentz (USGS) for many detailed and thoughtful comments and suggestions.

Coastal Change from Hurricane Sandy and the 2012–13 Winter Storm Season: Fire Island, New York

By Cheryl J. Hapke, Owen Brenner, Rachel Hehre, and B.J. Reynolds

Abstract

The U.S. Geological Survey (USGS) mounted a substantial effort in response to Hurricane Sandy including an assessment of the morphological impacts to the beach and dune system at Fire Island, New York. Field surveys of the beach and dunes collected just prior to and after landfall were used to quantify change in several focus areas. In order to quantify morphologic change along the length of the island, pre-storm (May 2012) and post-storm (November 2012) lidar and aerial photography were used to assess changes to the shoreline and beach, and to measure volumetric changes. The extent and thicknesses of overwash deposits were mapped in the field, and measurements were used to determine volume, distribution, and characteristics of the deposits.

The beaches and dunes on Fire Island were severely eroded during Hurricane Sandy, and the island breached in three locations on the eastern segment of the island. Landward shift of the upper portion of the beach averaged 19.7 meters (m) but varied substantially along the coast. Shoreline change was also highly variable, but the shoreline prograded during the storm by an average of 11.4 m, due to the deposition of material eroded from the upper beach and dunes onto the lower portion of the beach. The beaches and dunes lost 54.4 percent of their pre-storm volume, and the dunes experienced overwash along 46.6 percent of the island. The inland overwash deposits account for 14 percent of the volume lost from the beaches and dunes, indicating that the majority of material was moved offshore.

In the winter months following Hurricane Sandy, seven storm events with significant wave heights greater than 4 m were recorded at a wave buoy 30 nautical miles (NM) south of Fire Island. Monthly shoreline and profile surveys indicate that the beach continued to erode dramatically. The shoreline, which exhibited a progradational trend immediately after Sandy, eroded an average of 21.4 m between November 2012 and mid-March 2013, with a maximum landward shift of nearly 60 m. By March 2013 the elevation of the beach in the majority of the surveyed profiles was lowered below the mean high water level (0.46 m), and the beach lost an additional 18.9 percent of its remaining volume. In the final time period of the field surveys (March to April 2013), the beach began to show signs of rapid recovery, and in 90 percent of the profiles, the volume of the beach in April 2013 was similar to the volume measured immediately after Hurricane Sandy.

Overall, Hurricane Sandy profoundly impacted the morphology of Fire Island and resulted in an extremely low elevation, low relief configuration that has left the barrier island vulnerable to future storms. The coastal system subsequently began to show signs of recovery, and although the beach is likely to experience continued recovery in the form of volume gains, the dunes will take years to rebuild. Events such as Sandy result in a coastal environment that is more vulnerable to future storm impacts, but they are an important natural process of barrier islands that allow these systems to evolve in response to sea-level rise.

Introduction

According to the National Hurricane Center, Hurricane Sandy, at nearly 2,000 kilometers (km) in diameter, is the largest storm on historical record in the Atlantic basin. The storm, which made landfall coincident with astronomical high tides, affected an extensive area of the east coast of the United States. The highest waves and storm surge were focused along the heavily populated New York and New Jersey coasts. The storm made landfall near Atlantic City, New Jersey, the evening of October 29, 2012. At the height of the storm, a record significant wave height of 9.6 m (m) was recorded at the wave buoy offshore of Fire Island, New York (fig. 1, inset). During the storm, beaches were severely eroded and dunes extensively overwashed. Fire Island was breached in three locations, and the coastal infrastructure, including many private residences, was heavily damaged (fig. 2).

The U.S. Geological Survey (USGS) has an ongoing coastal morphologic change and processes project at Fire Island, New York. One of the objectives of the project is to understand the morphologic evolution of the barrier system on a variety of time scales (storms-decades-century). Many studies that support these project objectives have been completed (Hapke and others, 2010; Lentz and Hapke, 2011; Kratzmann and Hapke, 2012; Lentz and others, 2013; Schwab and others, 2013); however, little information is available about storm-driven change in this region. The USGS, as part of the National Assessment of Coastal Change Hazards project, also conducts regional data collection and impact analyses in response to extreme storm events such as Sandy (*http://coastal.er.usgs.gov/hurricanes/*). As part of this effort, post-Sandy light detection and ranging (lidar) data and a series of along-coast oblique aerial photos were collected for Fire Island (Stockdon and others, 2013). In addition, a USGS field team conducted differential global positioning system (DGPS) surveys at Fire Island to quantify the morphologic state of the beach and dunes immediately prior to the storm. The area was re-surveyed immediately post-storm, as soon as access to the island was possible, as well as a number of times throughout the winter of 2012–13. The field surveys document the response of the system from Sandy's effects and the cumulative changes that resulted from a series of strong extra-tropical (nor'easter) storms.

The post-Sandy lidar data were used in conjunction with lidar data from May 2012 and DGPS surveys to conduct assessments of shoreline and upper beach change, examine morphologic change on profiles along the length of the island, and map overwash deposits. Pre- and post-Sandy lidar data were used to characterize changes to island morphology by extracting an upper beach contour parameter (U_b) to analyze the persistence and migration of higher elevations during the storm, and to extract pre- and post-storm profiles along the length of the island. DGPS surveys were used to measure the alongshore position and elevation of the beach in order to derive a mean high water (MHW) shoreline, and a temporally dense set of cross-shore profiles were collected to measure changes to the shape and volume of the beach and dunes in focus areas through the winter and spring. Additional field teams mapped the location and thickness of overwash deposits along the length of the island shortly after Hurricane Sandy. Combined with remote sensing data from pre-storm (May 2012) and post-storm (November 2012) lidar data and aerial photography, an overwash dataset was compiled to assess the role of overwash in the response of the island.

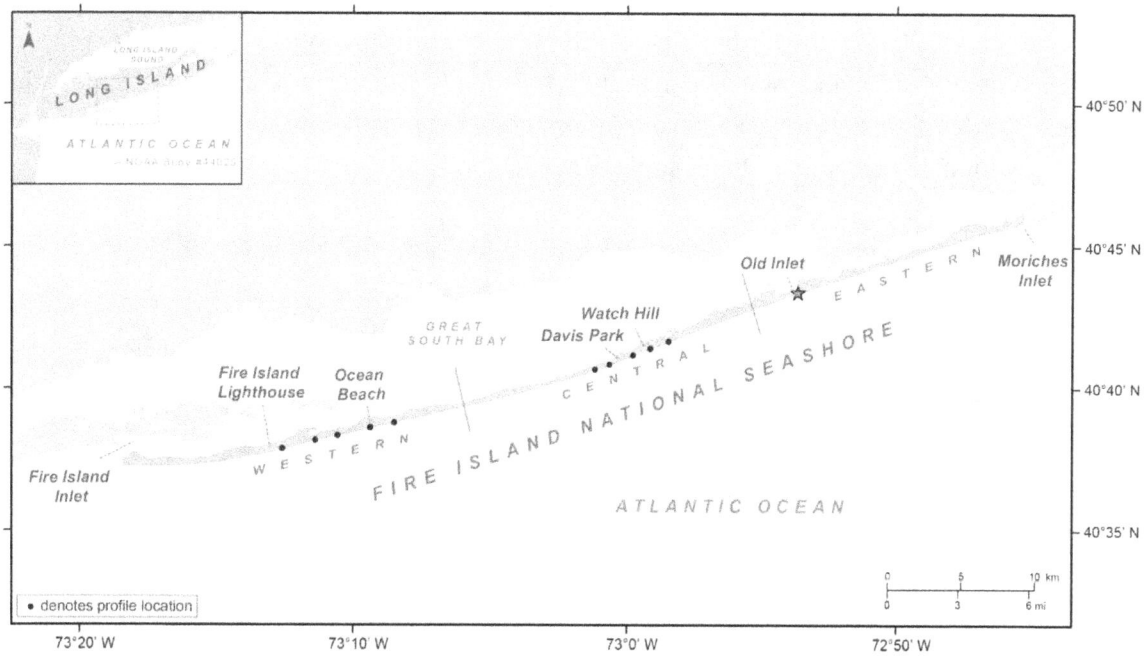

Figure 1. Location map of Fire Island, New York. The locations of the cross-shore DGPS profiles are marked by the dots, and alongshore DGPS surveys extend from Fire Island Lighthouse in the west to the breach at Old Inlet (star). Three subareas (western, central, and eastern) that correspond to subdivisions defined in previous studies (Lentz and others, 2013; Schwab and others, 2013) are also shown.

Methods

2.1. Cross-Shore Profiles

As part of the assessment of beach and dune morphologic change associated with Hurricane Sandy and the series of winter storms that followed, DGPS elevation data were collected along 10 shore-perpendicular profiles extending from just inland of the crest of the dune to the low-tide swash zone. Profile elevations were surveyed 1 day prior to landfall, over a period of 3 days immediately after the storm, and at monthly intervals for 5 months (table 1) to capture both the initial impact of the event and the ongoing recovery of the beach system. The spatial distribution and number of field-surveyed profiles are limited due to restrictions on access to the island immediately before and after Hurricane Sandy made landfall. Profile elevation data were collected at 0.5-second intervals using an Ashtech Z-Xtreme GPS surveying instrument and post-processed using positional data from a base receiver to achieve sub-decimeter accuracies. The profiles are located in two regions of Fire Island (western and central) to capture the storm response in areas that vary morphologically and geologically (Leatherman and Allen, 1985; Lentz and others, 2013; Schwab and others, 2013). These profiles were used to assess relative changes to dune, beach, and swash zone morphology and to calculate beach volume and volume change. Beach volumes were calculated by integrating the area below each profile using the lowest elevation value common to all surveys at each profile.

Figure 2.   Photos of Fire Island 2 to 4 days after Sandy made landfall: a) leveled beaches and scarped dunes in central Fire Island; b) houses undermined and destroyed at Davis Park; c) leveled dunes and large overwash sheets near Fire Island lighthouse; and d) the island breach at Old Inlet.

Table 1. Dates, types of surveys, and metrics collected or extracted for Hurricane Sandy and winter storm season change measurements, May 2012–April 2013.

Date	Survey type	Metric
May 7, 2012	topographic lidar	Shoreline, upper beach
Oct. 28, 2012	field survey	Profiles, shoreline
Nov. 2, 2012	field survey	Profiles, shoreline
Nov. 4, 2012	field survey	Profiles
Nov. 5, 2012	topographic lidar	Shoreline, upper beach
Dec. 1, 2012	field survey	Profiles, shoreline
Dec. 12, 2012	field survey	Profiles, shoreline
Jan. 10, 2013	field survey	Profiles, shoreline
Feb. 12, 2013	field survey	Profiles, shoreline
Mar. 13, 2013	field survey	Profiles, shoreline
Apr. 9, 2013	field survey	Profiles, shoreline

2.2 Shoreline Change

In conjunction with the recurrent cross-shore profile surveys, continuous alongshore DGPS data were collected to assess the positional changes of the MHW shoreline and the upper portion of the beach. Data were collected along shore-parallel tracks to capture the base of the dune, the mid-beach, and the upper and lower foreshore. The alongshore tracks extend from just west of Fire Island Lighthouse (fig. 1) to the western flank of the storm-induced inlet breach at Old Inlet.

The MHW shoreline (0.46 m North American Vertical Datum of 1988 [NAVD 88]; Weber and others, 2005) is derived from the field data by using an interpolation method that creates a series of equally-spaced cross-shore profiles between the two survey lines that flank the MHW contour. The foreshore slope is assumed to be uniform on each profile. Using this slope and the two surveyed positions on each cross-shore profile, a simple geometric calculation is done to find where each profile line intersects the MHW contour.

The migration of the shoreline through time is assessed by quantifying the net shoreline movement (NSM) over different time periods by using the interpolated shorelines and 50 m-spaced transects in the Digital Shoreline Analysis System (DSAS; Thieler and others, 2009).

2.3. Lidar Data

To characterize morphologic change over a larger spatial extent than the field profiles allow, additional profile elevations were extracted from May 7, 2012, and post-storm

(November 5, 2012) lidar datasets (Stockdon and others, 2013) at 42 cross-shore locations covering the length of Fire Island. The locations of these profiles correspond to those from an ongoing study prior to Hurricane Sandy (see fig. 5 for profile locations). Volumes for each profile were calculated by using area integration methods described in section 2.1, and net volume change was assessed for each profile.

Qualitative assessments were conducted to verify that the May 2012 lidar data adequately represent a "pre-storm" beach. There were relatively minor variations in profile morphology and elevation between the May 2012 and the October 28, 2012, field surveys, and the differences were primarily concentrated on the lower portion of the beach (below 2.5 m). The pre-storm (October 28) field profile tends to have a slightly higher upper beach surface and more developed berm with a steeper beachface than in May 2012, which likely developed over the 5+ summer months between surveys (fig. 3). Although the May 2012 lidar survey does not represent an immediate pre-storm dataset, differences between the field and the lidar surveys are minimal, and the assessment is included due to the value gained by the extended spatial coverage provided by the lidar dataset.

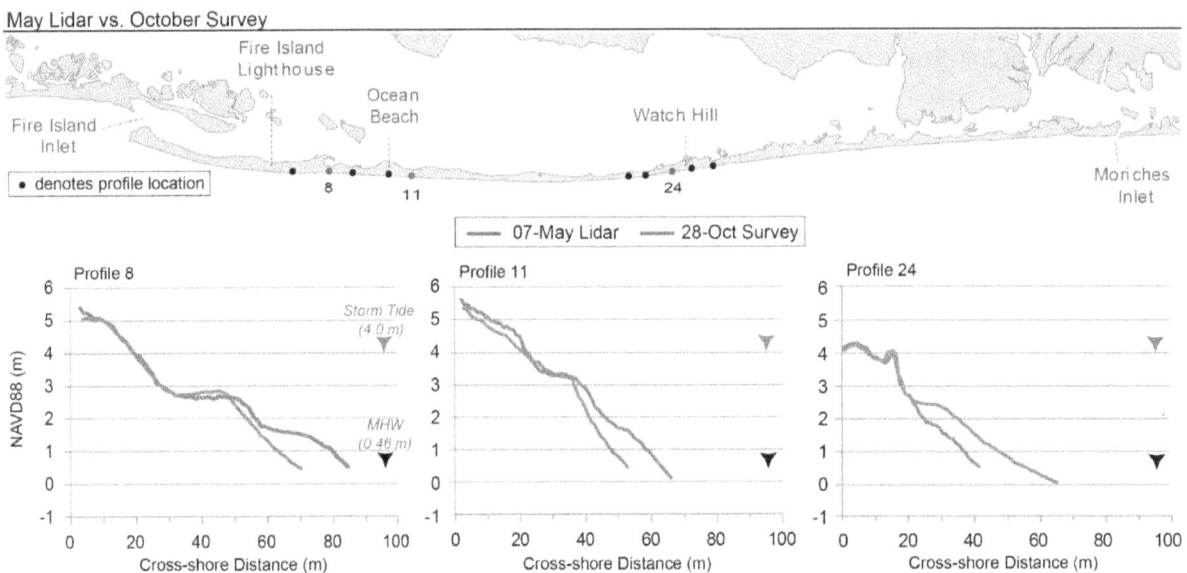

Figure 3.   Comparisons of pre-Sandy beach profiles from lidar data (May 5, 2012) and field survey (Oct. 28, 2013) at three survey profile locations in western and central Fire Island.

2.4. Upper Beach Change

The widespread occurrence of overwash on Fire Island resulted in the leveling or removal of the dune in many places (fig. 2). Quantifying the storm impact to the upper beach and dunes becomes problematic where the dune no longer exists as part of the post-storm system.

In order to evaluate changes to the dune zone, even in areas where this morphologic feature has been removed, a spatially persistent upper beach elevation contour (U_b; 2.9 m) was identified. This parameter provides a way to quantify the magnitude of the impact to the dune zone. The horizontal migration of U_b between May 2012 and November 2012 was calculated using the DSAS, and amounts of U_b change were compared to the MHW shoreline migration values (Stockdon and others, 2013). For the whole-island assessments, the U_b and the MHW shoreline were derived from May 2012 and post-storm lidar data.

2.5. Overwash Volumes

Overwash during storms typically carries substantial volumes of sand to the interior and back-bay areas of barrier islands. In developed and populated areas, the sand deposited along houses, yards, sidewalks, and roads is often bulldozed to clear access shortly after a storm. In some cases this sand is relocated to the approximate location of the pre-storm dune. The bulldozing activity disturbs or removes the natural deposit, erasing the record of volume and distribution. To estimate the immediate post-storm overwash volumes from Hurricane Sandy for all of Fire Island, a combination of field, remote sensing, and GIS analytical techniques was used. A group of ground-based National Park Service (NPS) volunteers surveyed 50 overwash fans following a protocol developed by the USGS field team to create an unusually large and detailed dataset of storm overwash deposit thicknesses.

The thickness of each deposit was measured along a transect near the center of the deposit and around the perimeter by digging down until a vegetation horizon (assumed to be the pre-storm surface) was encountered and measuring the thickness from the vegetation horizon to the surface of the deposit. The boundaries of each fan and the locations of the thickness measurements were mapped using a handheld GPS. The fans were mapped within a week following Sandy with a focus on the developed areas first to obtain measurements prior to the bulldozing of the washover deposits to clear roads and provide access. Post-storm aerial imagery (National Oceanic and Atmospheric Administration, 2013), taken 6 days after the storm (November 4, 2012) was used to visually verify the areal extent of the fans and to delineate any unmapped fans. Seventy-three percent of the washover deposits (by area) were mapped in the field, and the remainder—generally small, isolated deposits—were mapped using remote sensing techniques. The thicknesses of the unsampled fans were estimated based on nearby fan thickness measurements and relative elevations. A total of 797 thickness measurements were obtained and subsequently used to create isopach surfaces using interpolation techniques. Volumes for each deposit were calculated from the isopach surfaces.

Results and Discussion

3.1. Profile Volume and Elevation

3.1.1 Effects of Hurricane Sandy

The nine DGPS profile surveys collected immediately prior to (October 28) and following (November 2 and 4) Hurricane Sandy demonstrate the substantial effects of the storm (figs. 4, 5; appendix 1). All profiles show a major decline in elevation and volume. Waves and storm surge carried large quantities of sand offshore and inland by way of overwash. The resulting post-storm profiles show wide, nearly flat beaches with little or no dunes remaining. The upper portion of the beach lost 1–3 m in elevation as the profile moved from a reflective morphology with a well-defined berm crest and steeply sloped beach face to a more dissipative or nearly flat beach surface (fig. 4). The primary dunes experienced considerable erosion and were removed entirely in 4 of the 10 surveyed profiles. All of the profiles that showed complete dune loss are within the developed communities (appendix 1, profiles 8–11, 24). During the 6 days surrounding the storm, volume decline for all profiles ranged from 22 to 53 percent with an average loss of 35.4 percent (table 2). Volume loss did not differ significantly between the western (7–11) and central profiles (22–26).

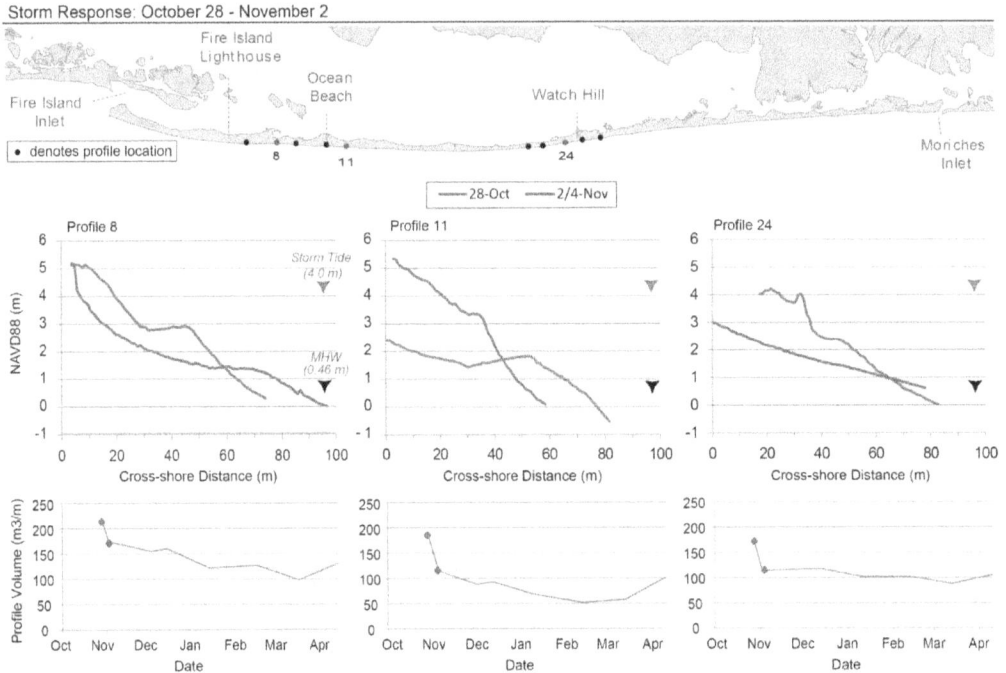

Figure 4. Examples of pre- and post-storm field profiles from three locations on Fire Island following Hurricane Sandy (Oct. 28–Nov. 2, 2012). Plots in lower panel show evolution of profile volume (in cubic meters per meter [m3/m]) throughout survey period. All profiles for all dates are provided in appendix 1.

The field surveys are limited in their spatial coverage, but they provide an important pre-storm baseline of the system just before landfall. Island-wide comparisons of the May and November (2012) profile elevations from the lidar surveys demonstrate extensive losses along the length of the island. The percentage of volume change calculated from the lidar profiles indicates an average loss of 54.4 percent, whereas the volume change calculated from the field surveys indicates an average volume loss of 35.4 percent (table 2). The higher percentage of loss measured with the lidar data as compared to field profiles reflects the inclusion of the highly impacted eastern end of the island in the lidar change calulations.

Table 2. Average profile-based percentage of volume change for three subregions and all-island as derived from GPS and lidar data.

[m, meter; m³/m, cubic meters per meter]

Average Percent Profile Volume Change (m³/m)				
Survey type	West	Central	East	All-island
Lidar (42)	−58.5 (12)	−47.8 (12)	−58.5 (10)	**−54.4**
Field (9)	−35.7(4)	−35.2 (5)		**−35.4**

() denotes the number of profiles used to make the measurement

In addition to the island-wide assessment, volume change variations were examined in three subregions (table 2) that correspond to variations in the underlying geology (Schwab and others, 2013). The volume loss in the west and east subregions was slightly (10 percent) greater than the volume loss in the central subregion, and the east subregion shows the greatest variability (fig. 5). Profiles in the east and west lost the greatest percentage of volume related to total or near-total removal of the dune and extensive overwash (for example, see appendix 1, profiles 9–11, 38, 40). Beaches in the central subregion tended to consistently show only moderate (1–3 m) dune and beach erosion and significantly less dune overwash.

Profiles located within the boundaries of a 2009 beach nourishment project (profiles 8–11, 18, 19, 23, and 24) indicate that areas in communities that were nourished experienced greater volume loss than profiles in non-nourished areas of the island (volume losses of 72.0 percent and 54.6 percent, respectively; table 3). Lower initial volumes in the nourished areas may be a function of lower dune volumes associated with development in the communities.

Table 3. Average initial volume and percent volume change for profiles within 2009 nourishment project area.

[m, meter; m³/m, cubic meters per meter]

Average Profile Volume Change		
Survey type	Initial volume (m³/m)	Percent change
Nourished (8)	94.3	−72.0
Non-Nourished (34)	160.7	−54.6

() denotes the number of profiles used to make the measurement

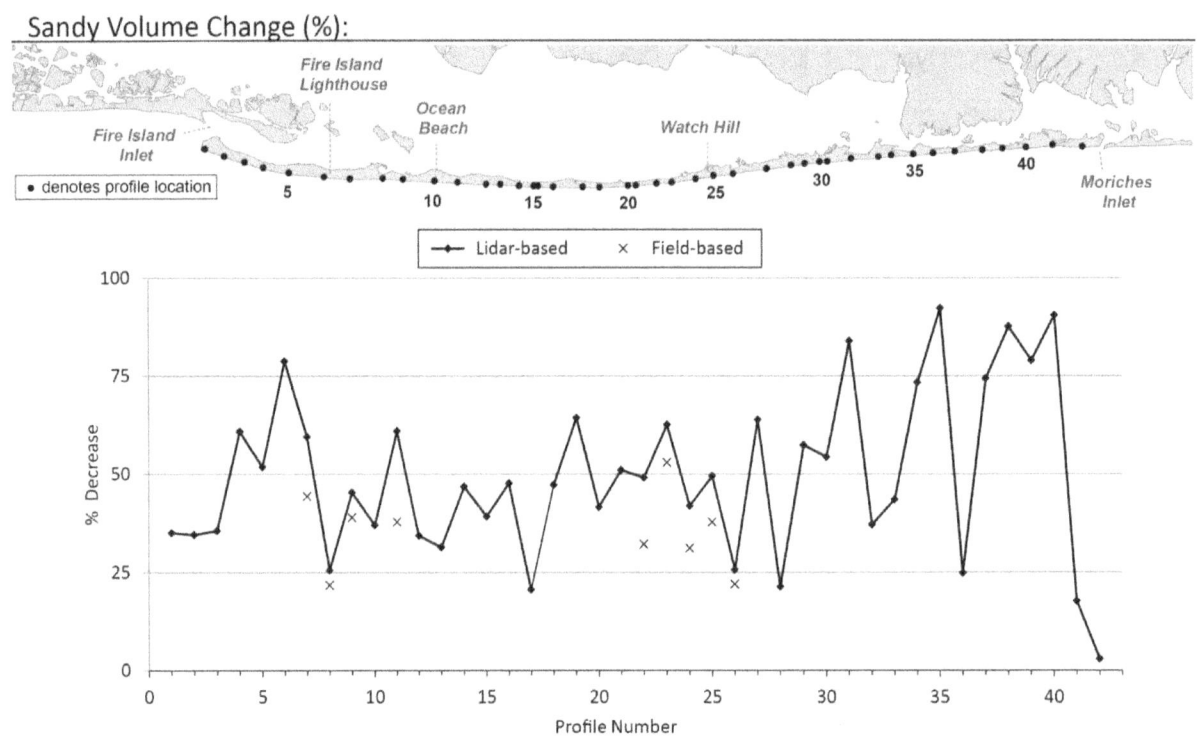

Figure 5. Alongshore profile volume loss values (%) derived from pre- and post-Sandy GPS (Oct. 28–Nov. 4, 2012) and lidar (May 7–Nov. 5, 2012) datasets. The lidar profile locations are shown on the map and correspond to a series of 45 along-coast profiles that were identified in a pre-Sandy study. Slightly lower volume change values in the GPS survey are due to losses that occurred between May 2012 and the October 28, 2012, field survey.

3.1.2 Post-Sandy Response and Recovery

In the winter months following Hurricane Sandy, a series of strong nor'easter storms (particularly those with ≥ 4 m deep-water wave height; fig. 6) caused additional beach and dune loss on Fire Island. The changes during the 2012–13 winter season that were documented during eight post-Sandy surveys include significant and continual fluctuations in beach morphology from November to April (fig. 7; appendix 1). Predominant morphologic change patterns were examined for the 10 field survey profiles (table 4).

Table 4. Differences in beach profile volume (percent change) between consecutive beach GPS profile surveys for western, central, and all locations, October 2012–April 2013. Positive values indicate profile volume gain, and negative values indicate volume loss.

	Incremental Average Volume Change (%)								
	28-Oct	2-Nov	4-Nov	1-Dec	12-Dec	10-Jan	12-Feb	13-Mar	9-Apr
West	–	−35.0	1.1	−9.6	−0.2	−22.3	2.5	−5.2	32.3
Central	–	−35.2	−0.4	−0.2	1.7	−13.7	4.9	0.4	5.6
ALL	–	−35.1	0.1	−4.4	0.7	−18.0	3.7	−2.4	18.9

Following the initial post-Sandy assessment (November 2–4), calmer deep-water wave conditions (except for one stronger storm event on November 8) allowed for reformation of the lower portion of the beach, as indicated by the December 12th survey (fig. 7) which shows building of the berm and steepening of the beach face. These changes are characteristic of post-storm recovery. However, the average profile volume still decreased by 4.4 percent across all surveyed locations during the month following Hurricane Sandy. Volumetric losses appear to be related to the seaward transfer of sand from the beach and dune to the lower beachface and surf zone (fig. 7).

From December 12 to January 10, profiles at all 10 survey locations (appendix 1) show substantial erosional behavior as beach recovery from the prior month is reversed. The largest post-Sandy nor'easter occurred during this time period (December 26–27), with significant wave heights reaching over 7 m (fig. 6). Beach elevations were lowered by as much as 1.5 m. By January 10, the beaches had lost an average of 18 percent of their remaining volume, and 4 of the 10 profile locations exhibited a volumetric minimum. Average beach elevation slightly increased in the February 12 surveys, primarily along the lower beachface.

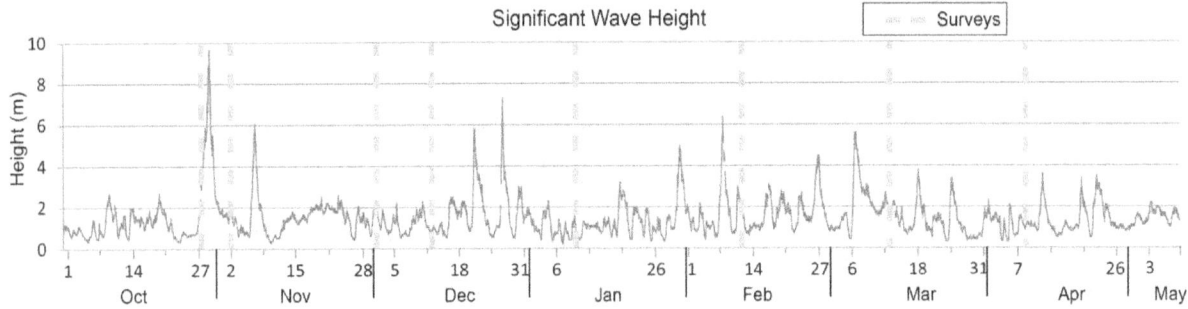

Figure 6. Deep water wave heights (H$_s$) during hurricane Sandy (October 28–29, 2012) and seven post-Sandy winter storms (wave heights > 4 m) as recorded at wave buoy positioned approximately 30NM south of Islip, NY (National Oceanographic and Atmospheric Administration: National Data Buoy Center, Station #44025).

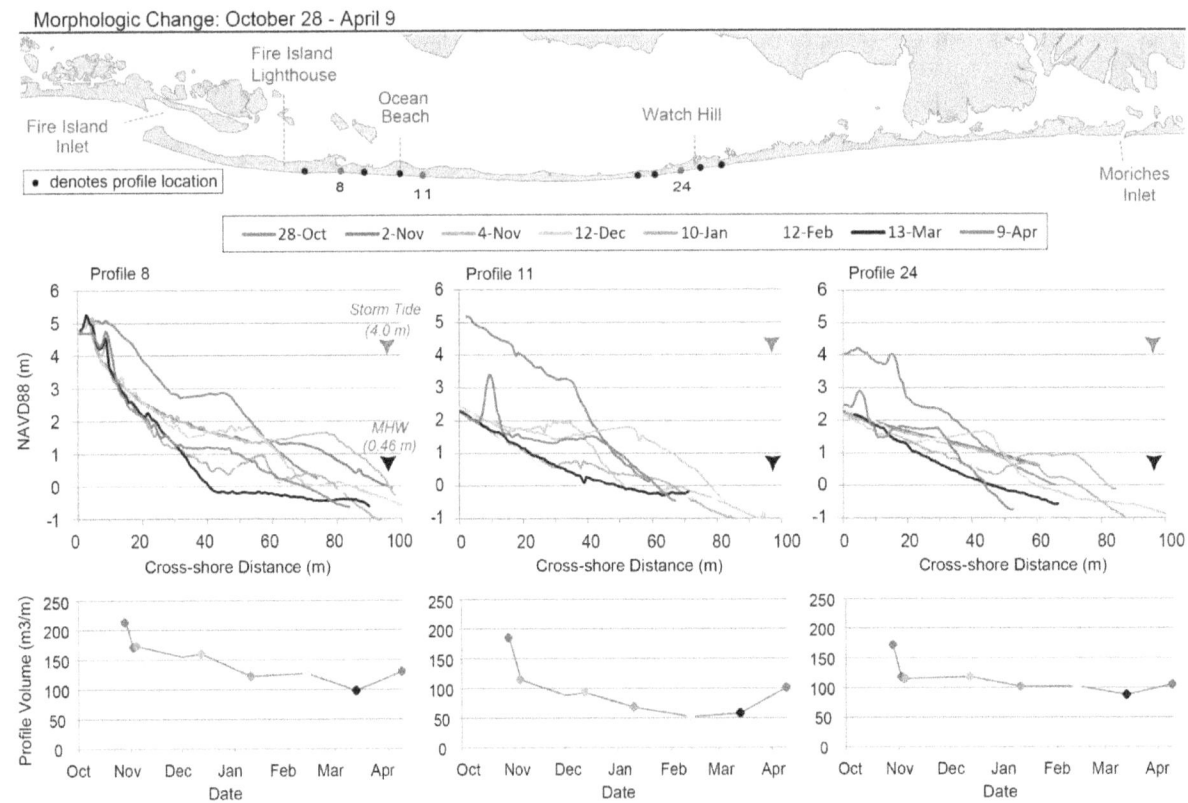

Figure 7. Examples of field profiles from three locations showing morphologic change from Hurricane Sandy and the winter of 2012–13 (Oct. 28, 2012–April 9, 2013). Artificial reconstruction of the dune is evident as early as the January 10, 2012 survey. All DGPS profiles for all dates are provided in appendix 1.

The subaerial portion of the beach underwent substantial change between March and April 2013 (fig. 7; table 4; appendix 1). Prolonged periods of high winter wave conditions in late February and early March led to decreases in lower beach elevation of up to 1.5 m in the March 13 survey. Beach response varied substantially with some areas (profiles 7, 11, 25, and 26) increasing in volume by as much as 26 percent and other areas (profiles 8, 9, and 24) reaching the lowest elevations and volumes of the study (figs. 7, 8; appendix 1). The beach and dunes showed measureable recovery by April 9 with beach width and elevation increasing substantially. Average volume increase of 18.9 percent occurred as the berm reformed and dune ramps began to rebuild along the upper beach. The widespread beach recovery coincides with a period of calmer wave conditions. Despite the end-of-winter recovery, however, the overall beach volume was 7 percent less than the post-Sandy measurement (November 2) and nearly 41 percent less than the pre-Sandy condition 23 weeks earlier (table 4; figs. 7, 8, 9).

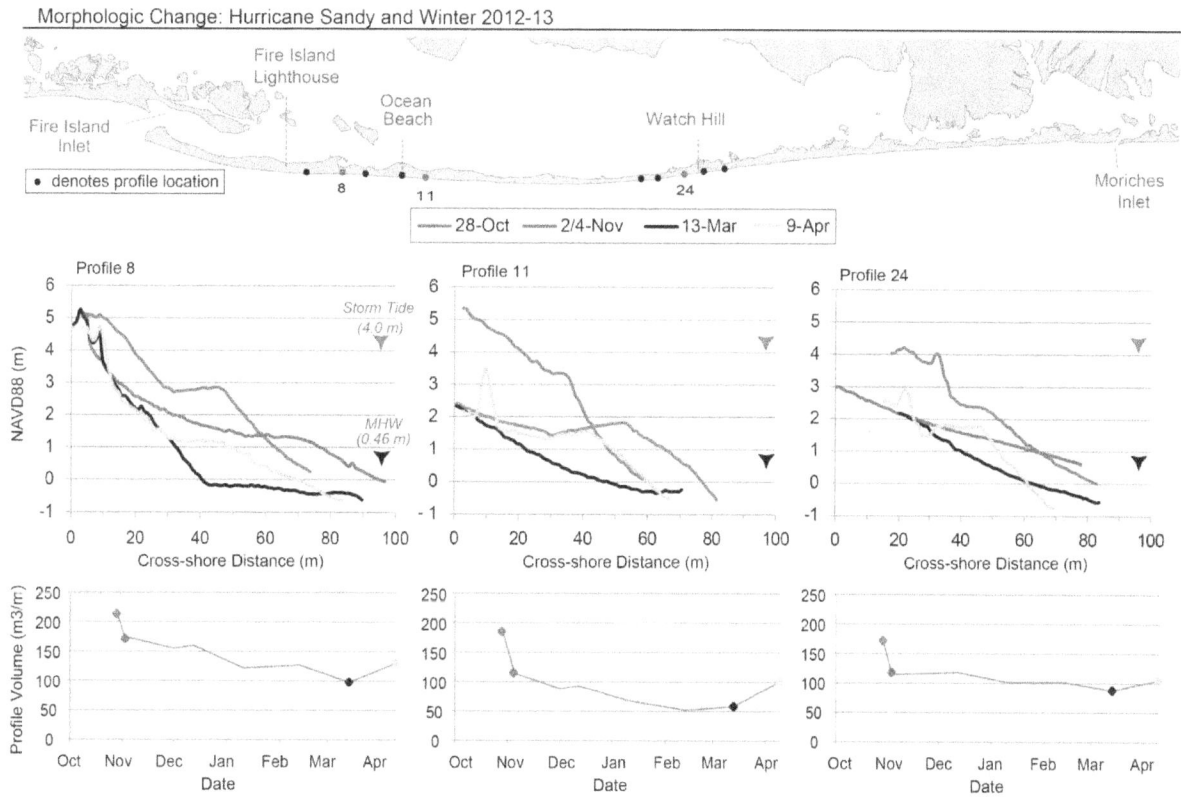

Figure 8. Examples of progressive changes in beach morphology from October 28, 2012, to April 9, 2013, with associated profile volumes (in cubic meters per meter [m³/m]) shown in lower panel. Following major Sandy loss, profiles continued to lose elevation and volume through March before experiencing slight gains in late March and early April.

13

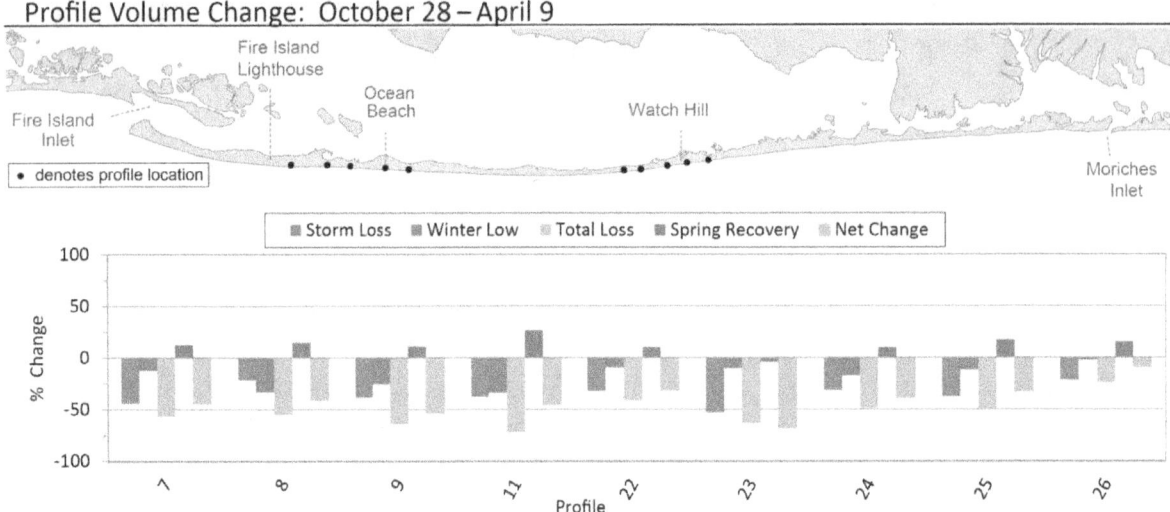

Figure 9. Observed trends in volume change (percentage of initial pre-storm volume) at GPS profile locations: Sandy loss (Oct. 28 to Nov. 2, 2012), winter low (Nov. 2 to lowest recorded volume), total loss (Oct. 28 to lowest volume), spring recovery (lowest volume to April 9, 2013), and net volume change (Oct. 28 to Apr. 9). Despite slight increase in volume and elevation at eight of nine profiles during March and April 2013, net volume change averages –40% from large storm losses and nearly continuous decline until the March 2013 survey.

3.2 Shoreline Change

3.2.1 Hurricane Sandy Movement

Net shoreline movement derived from the alongshore GPS surveys collected in the western and central subregions of Fire Island (fig. 1) indicates that between October 28 and November 2, the shoreline prograded (table 5; fig. 10). The gain of material in the foreshore (along the MHW contour) is attributable to material eroded from the beach and dunes during the storm and deposited on the lower portion of the beach or just offshore where it rapidly welded to the lower beach in the days after the storm (fig. 4). The net shoreline movement following Sandy was progradational and averaged 4.3 m, but movement was highly variable along the beach, with values ranging from +30.9 m to –25.9 m (table 5).

Table 5. Average and maximum values of shoreline change associated with Hurricane Sandy, the winter storm period, and total duration of the survey along 35 kilometers of Fire Island from Fire Island Lighthouse to the storm-induced inlet breach site in Old Inlet vicinity.

Time period		Accretion		Erosion	
	Avg (m)	Max (m)	Avg (m)	Max (m)	Avg (m)
Hurricane Sandy *(October 28, 2012–November 1 and 2, 2012)*	4.3	30.9	10.7	−25.9	−10.6
Winter *(November 1 and 2, 2012–March 2013)*	−21.4	41.0	12.6	−57.5	−24.1
Total change *(October 28, 2012–April 2013)*	−8.0	24.1	7.9	−63.6	−14.9

The patterns of shoreline change that resulted from Hurricane Sandy display a nearly sinusoidal pattern of alternating erosion and progradation cells in the western subregion (fig. 10A), with a length-scaling of approximately 1 km. In the central subregion, the shoreline response to Sandy was also largely progradational and variable along the coast, although with a less distinct sinusoidal pattern than that mapped along western Fire Island (fig. 10B).

3.2.2 Winter Storm Season Response and Recovery

In the months following Hurricane Sandy, continued widespread and substantial erosion of the highly deflated and low-relief post-Sandy beach made the shoreline more vulnerable to the ensuing coastal storms. During the course of the winter months (November 4–March 13), the average change in the net movement of the shoreline was –21.4 m (table 5), with a maximum landward shift of nearly 60 m. Although some recovery of the shoreline was observed during the final survey period (April 7), many areas continued erode. During the 5 months of shoreline surveys (October 28–March 13) net shoreline movement averaged –8 m, with a maximum shoreline erosion value of 63.6 m (table 5). Similar to the pre- and post-Sandy surveys, net shoreline movement was variable, but with no distinct patterns of change (fig. 10).

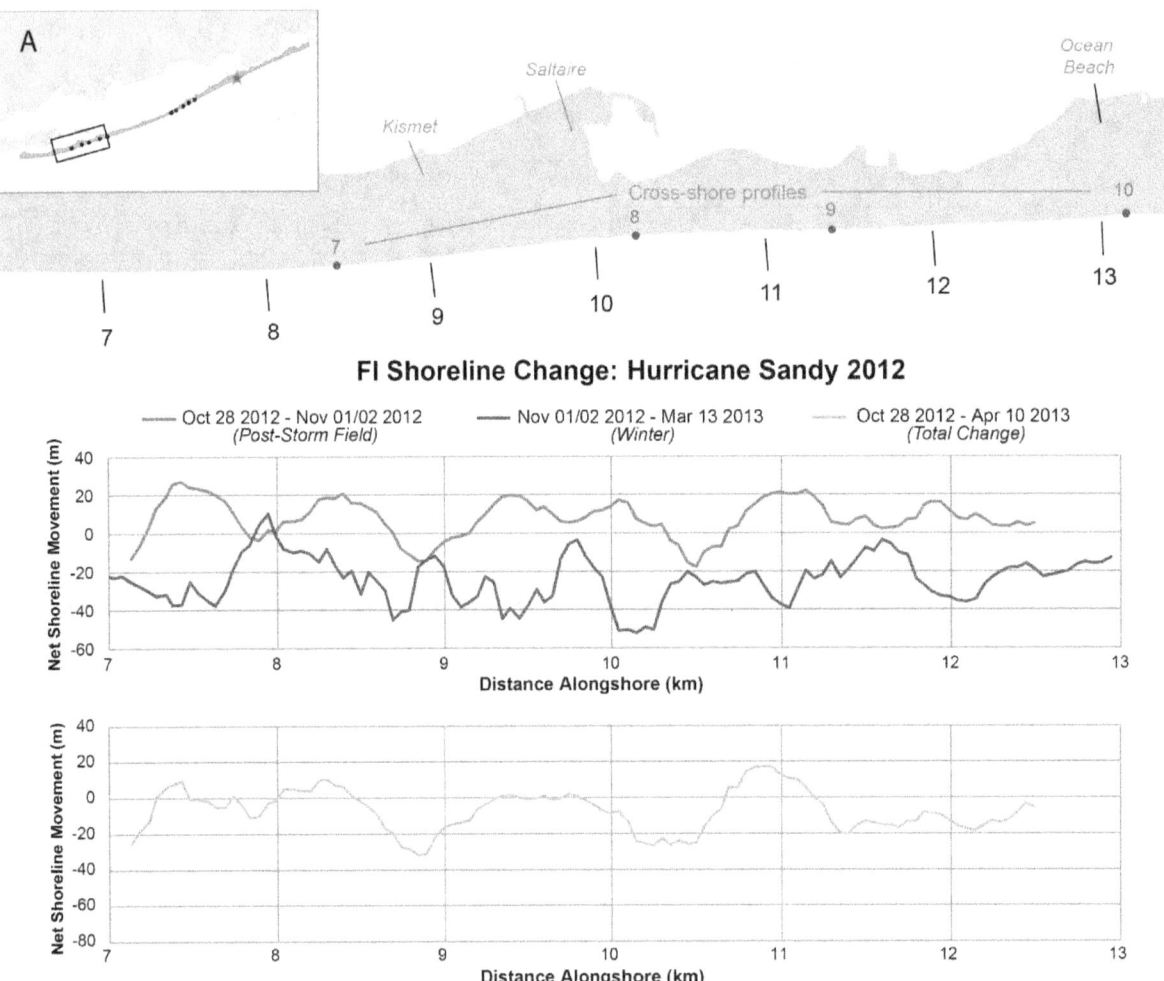

Figure 10. Net shoreline movement from Oct 28–Nov. 2 (blue line), Nov. 2–Mar. 13 (red line), and over the duration of the field surveys (Oct. 28–Apr. 9; green line) for (A) western Fire Island and (B) central Fire Island. See Figure 1 for survey coverage extents.

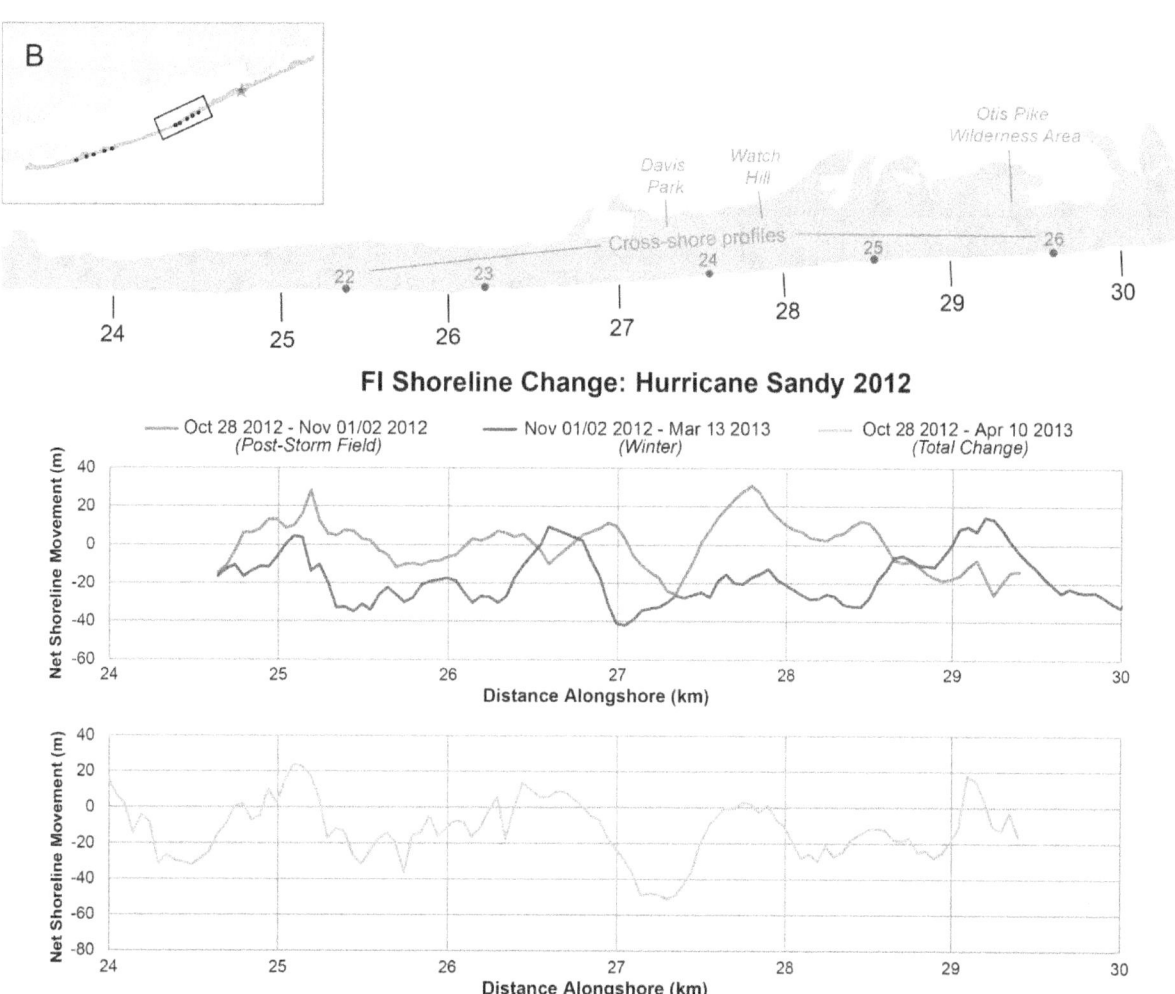

Figure 10—Continued. Net shoreline movement from Oct 28–Nov. 2 (blue line), Nov. 2–Mar. 13 (red line), and over the duration of the field surveys (Oct. 28–Apr. 9; green line) for (A) western Fire Island and (B) central Fire Island. See Figure 1 for survey coverage extents.

3.3 Upper Beach Change (U_b)

For this analysis, the upper beach (U_b) contour of 2.9 m consistently captures changes to the upper portion of the beach and dune system, including areas that experienced low to moderate overwash and areas where the dune was eroded and scarped but not overwashed (fig. 11). In several locations along the eastern end of Fire Island, severe overwash or breaching reduced the maximum elevation to below 2.9 m, resulting in data gaps where U_b does not exist (figs. 11A and 11C). Similar to the other methods used to characterize storm impacts, the U_b parameter is influenced by development, particularly where structures conceal the contour location. Additionally, U_b is obstructed in areas where infrastructure is found seaward of the pre-storm dune line (such as Davis Park).

17

Based on the landward movement of U_b from May 2012 to post-storm (Nov 5, 2012) lidar data, the western subregion of Fire Island had the greatest erosion of the upper portion of the beach where large areas of overwash account for as much as 100 m of landward movement, with an average of –25.1 m (table 6). Erosion of U_b was substantially less along both central and eastern Fire Island. Along the central portion of the island, storm impacts were comparatively lower than to the east and west. In eastern Fire Island, the lower net retreat of U_b is likely a function of the narrower initial island width and lower elevation that allowed for multiple occurrences of overwash extending across the island to the bay. A more complete U_b migration assessment on Fire Island was hindered by the breach and alongshore variety in overwash scenarios which made the selection of a constant island-wide U_b elevation difficult.

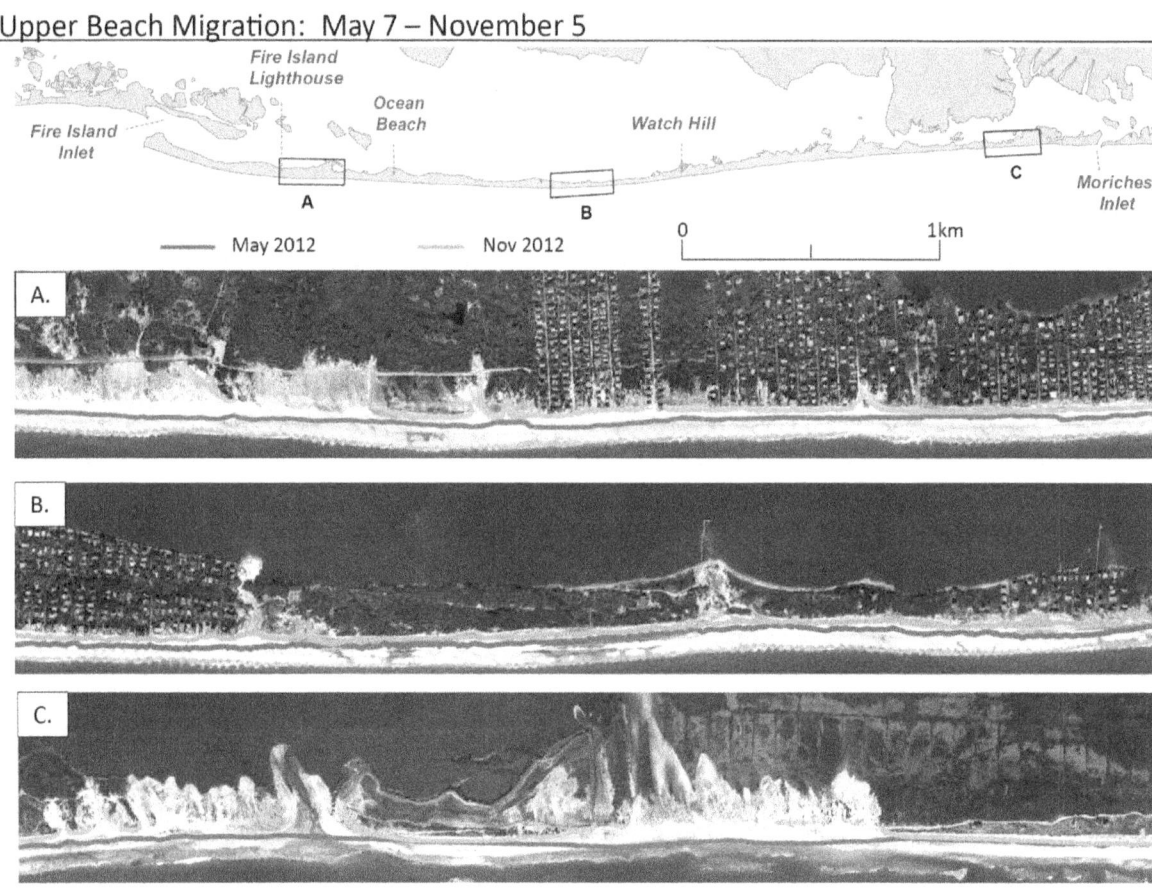

Figure 11.　Post-storm aerial images showing alongshore patterns in storm overwash and upper beach (U_b) migration of Fire Island, New York, from May 7, 2012, (purple line) to November 5, 2012 (orange line). Wide, continuous overwash along the western portion of the island (A) accounts for greater U_b migration values, while infrequent, narrow overwash deposits in the central region (B) result in less U_b migration on average. Extensive overwash along western and eastern Fire Island (A and C) reduces maximum cross-shore elevations below the U_b elevation, resulting in data gaps.

Table 6. Average alongshore U_b, shoreline and percent profile volume change among profiles within three geologic regions and all of Fire Island, New York.

[U_b, upper beach contour parameter; m, meter; m³/m, cubic meters per meter; %, percent; Δ, change]

	U_b (m)	Shoreline (m)	% Vol. Δ (m³/m)
West	−25.1	9.3	−58.5
Central	−20.6	13.2	−49.6
East	−14.0	11.0	−58.5
All island	**−19.7**	**11.4**	**−54.5**

To assess the storm impacts on the upper and lower beach systems, we examined the net change associated with the shoreline and U_b along the length of the island from May to November 2012 (fig. 12). Similar to the shoreline response from the field surveys, the all-island shoreline change is predominantly progradational. Based on field observations and quantification of overwash volumes, substantial amounts of material from the beaches and dunes were carried offshore during the storm. In the days immediately following the storm, substantial amounts of material were deposited along the lower portion of the beach. Although the beach was significantly reduced in elevation (fig. 4; appendix 1), the deposition of material along the lower beach produced an overall accretional "storm" trend of the shoreline.

Areas that experienced higher amounts of landward migration of U_b (e.g. western Fire Island) appear to correspond to areas where shoreline progradation is lower. Conversely, areas where U_b experienced lesser amounts of landward migration (such as central Fire Island) have higher magnitudes of shoreline progradation. This relationship appears to be a function of the dune size—in areas with lower dunes and more prone to overwash, there was more landward transport of material, resulting in lower values for shoreline progradation. In areas with larger dunes and less prone to overwash, material eroded from the dune was deposited lower on the beach, resulting in progradation.

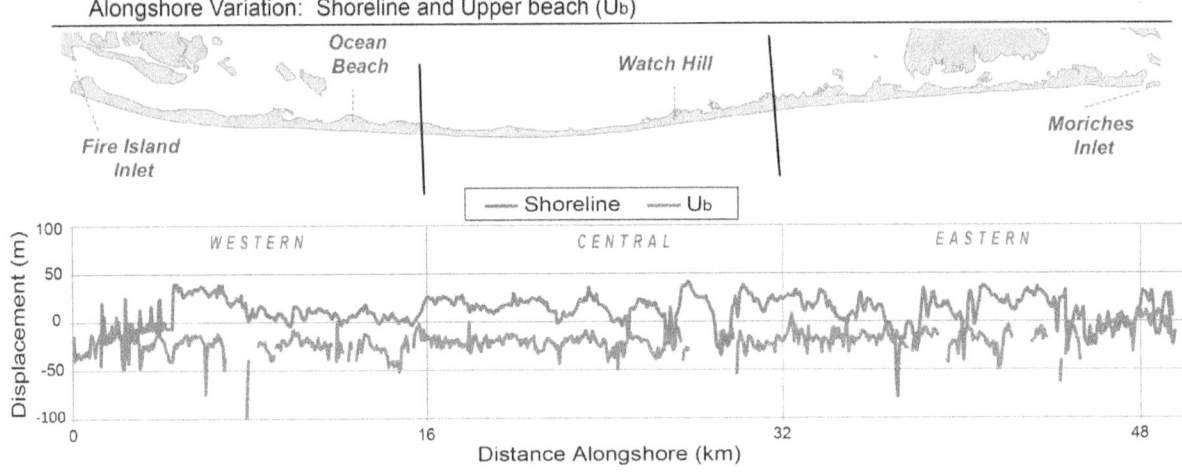

Alongshore Variation: Shoreline and Upper beach (Ub)

Figure 12. Variations in total shoreline (SL) and upper beach (Ub) migration (in meters) caused by Hurricane Sandy calculated from pre-storm (May 7, 2012) and post-storm (November 5, 2012) lidar data. Widespread overwash and erosion reduce island topography such that shoreline position tends to move seaward while Ub migrates landward in all three subregions of Fire Island, New York. Gaps in Ub data result from erosion elimination of the Ub contour elevations along the cross-shore profile during Hurricane Sandy.

3.4 Overwash

Overwash of the dunes from Hurricane Sandy, mapped by using data from field surveys and aerial imagery, occurred along 41 percent of the length of Fire Island (fig. 13). Field measurements of deposit thickness were used to estimate the volume of each continuous deposit, with an estimated 509,354 cubic meters (m^3) of material transported inland of the primary dune (table 7). The total volume lost from the beaches and dunes, estimated from island-wide profile volume decreases, was 3,500,000 m^3, indicating that overwash accounts for approximately 14 percent of the total volume lost from the subaerial system, with the remainder likely transported offshore.

In addition to the above totals, table 7 provides the total area and volume of overwash and average deposit thickness for the western, central, and eastern subregions. Comparisons of the area, volume, and characteristics of overwash deposits demonstrate a varied response in the three subregions (figs. 14, 15). In the western portion of the island, overwash produced washover sheets rather than fans and surge channels, resulting in laterally continuous deposits (0.5–1 km alongshore) and associated continuous leveling of the dunes (figs. 13A and 14A). The incursion distance of the overwash sheets along western Fire Island was limited in many locations by private homes and other community infrastructure in the developed stretches of coast.

In the central subregion of Fire Island, the occurrence of overwash is relatively low and is confined to narrow (<100 m) channels that coincide with existing cuts (vehicle access points or other lows) in the otherwise continuous dunes (figs. 13B, 14B, 15B). Volumes of overwash are also significantly lower in the central subregion (Table 7), suggesting higher overall dune and island elevations and (or) lower waves and storm surge along this segment of the island compared to adjacent areas.

Eastern Fire Island experienced the greatest amount of overwash and inundation based on areal extent and volume of overwash deposits. In areas with high pre-Sandy dunes, surge channels cut through the dunes and carried large volumes of material to the island interior, deposited as overwash fans. In lower-lying portions of this subregion, continuous overwash fans and fields of overlapping overwash tongues extend across the width of the barrier island in many locations (figs. 13C, 14C, 15C). The eastern portion of the island was breached in three locations during Hurricane Sandy.

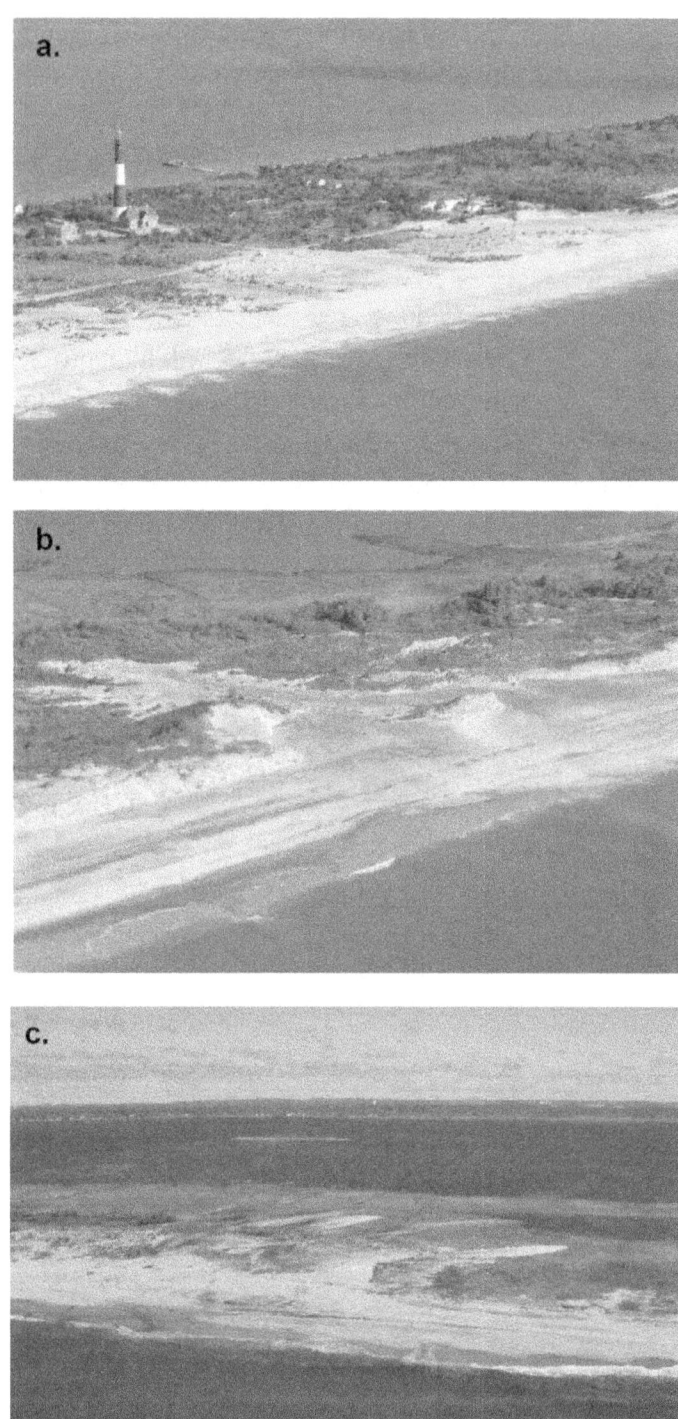

Figure 13. Examples of overwash styles at Fire Island, New York: (a) sheet wash in front of Fire Island Lighthouse, (b) surge channels through dunes and overwash fan along central-eastern Fire Island, and (c) tongues of overwash in eastern Fire Island.

Table 7. Total overwash area, volume, and average depth within three subregions and all of Fire Island, New York.

[m, meter; m², square meters; m³/m, cubic meters per meter]

	Area (m²)	Volume (m³)	Mean thickness (m)
West	598,083	189,812	0.32
Central	129,233	33,494	0.26
East	893,672	286,048	0.32
Total	**1,620,988**	**509,354**	**0.30**

Overwash Thickness:

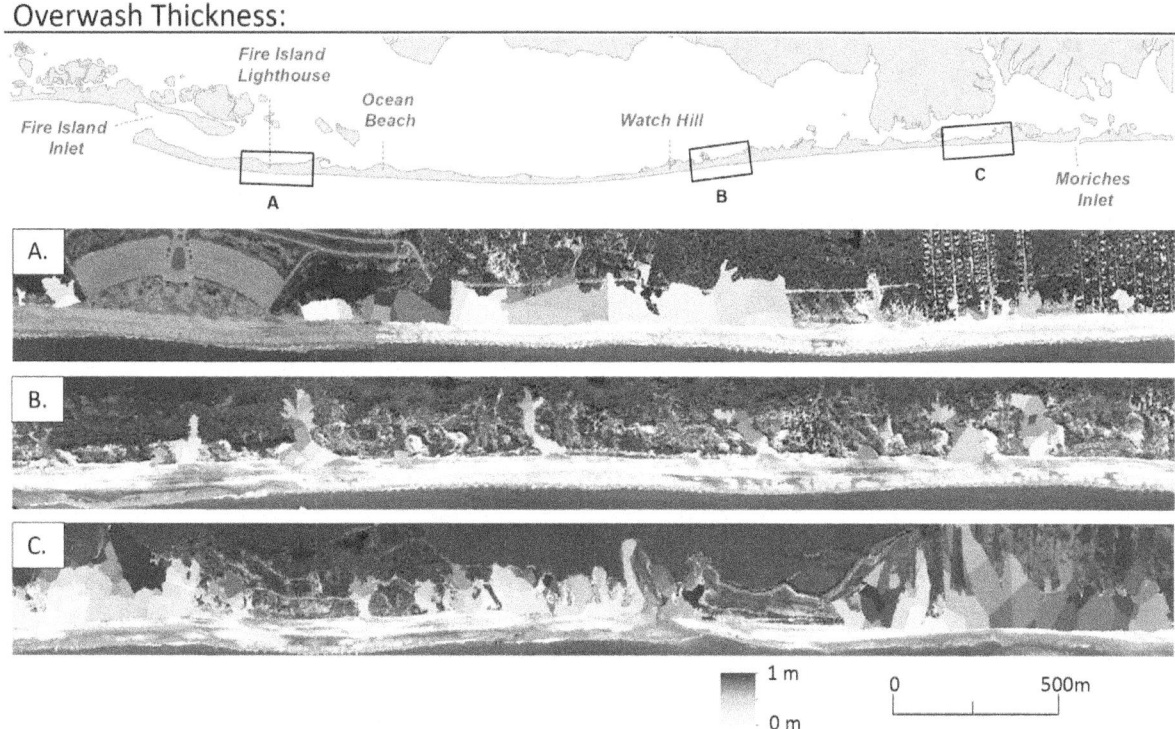

Figure 14. Isopach maps of overwash deposits resulting from Hurricane Sandy showing alongshore variation in size, density, and thickness. (A) Western and (C) eastern Fire Island, New York, have more laterally extensive overwash than the (B) central portion of the island.

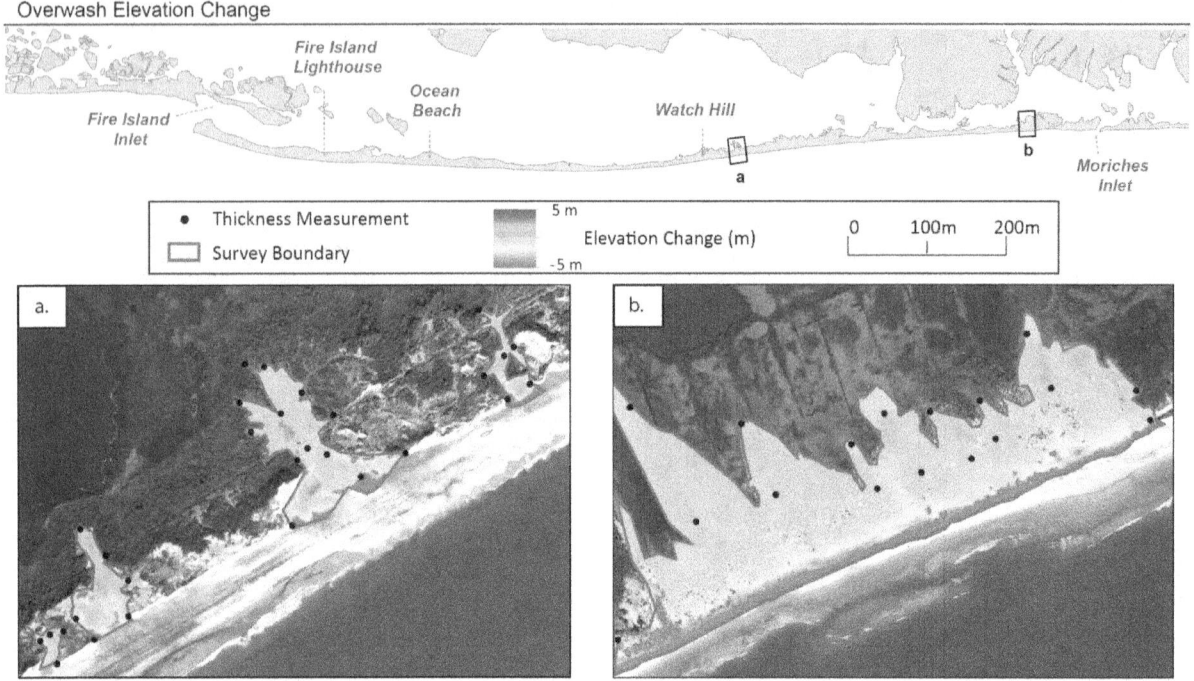

Figure 15. Net elevation change (in meters) associated (a) with narrow surge channels along central Fire Island, New York and (b) across a wide overwash field in the eastern subregion. Spatial elevation change data are derived from pre- and post-Sandy lidar surveys; point markers show distribution of field survey sample locations.

3.5 Summary of Overwash and Upper Beach Changes

There is a demonstrable along-coast variation in the morphologic response to Hurricane Sandy along Fire Island. The landward displacement of the U_b parameter and the volumes of overwash have a similar pattern of variation (figs. 11 and 14) that corresponds to documented variations in pre-storm elevation and along-island morphologic subsections. Areas with lower dune elevation and beach slope (western and eastern Fire Island) were severely overwashed and had greater overwash volumes (≥ 12 cubic meters per kilometer [m^3/km]) and higher U_b migration values than areas with higher dune elevation and beach slope. In areas of the island with higher pre-Sandy elevation and steeper beach slope (central Fire Island), overwash was confined to existing low elevations in the dune. In areas that did overwash, comparable amounts of volume loss occurred on the beaches and dunes; however, the U_b had lower amounts of inland migration, and overwash volumes were typically less than 5–6 m^3/km.

Despite coverage gaps for the U_b parameter and overwash field observations, both techniques provide realistic alongshore quantification of storm impact magnitude and the nature of morphologic change. Post-Sandy overwash data offer a means for comparing estimates of total island volume loss from profile data (~3,500,000 m^3) with total landward overwash deposition (~500,000 m^3). While data gaps tend to overlap with many of the most heavily

24

affected portions of Fire Island (such as breach zones) and limit accurate comparisons of regional U_b migration values, U_b migration measurements capture drastic beachface erosion and landward repositioning of the island during Hurricane Sandy.

Summary

Hurricane Sandy fundamentally changed the morphologic configuration of Fire Island, New York. Massive amounts of sand were carried to the interior of the island, into Great South Bay, or were moved offshore, and the island was breached in three locations. Post-Sandy measurements of volume loss of the beach and dunes indicated that on average the system lost 54.4 percent of its pre-storm volume. Nearly half (46.6%) of Fire Island was overwashed. In locations where the dunes were not fully breached, they eroded landward by as much as 36 m (22 m on average). The elevation of the beach was lowered by as much as 3 m. A parameter representing the typically more stable upper beach elevation (U_b) migrated 19.7 m landward on average and as much as 100 m in areas of severe cross-island overwash. The total estimated volume of overwash deposits represents 14 percent of the total volume lost from the subaerial beach and dune system.

Overall, the subregional variation in response, both from Sandy and from the series of nor'easter storms that occurred during the winter of 2012–13, suggests the island may be influenced by the regional geology and morphologic character of the inner continental shelf as described in recent literature (Hapke and others, 2010; Lentz and Hapke, 2011; Schwab and others, 2013). Eastern Fire Island had higher amounts of dune overwash, more landward displacement of the beach and U_b, and greater elevation loss of the beach and dune than central and western Fire Island. The morphologic effect on western Fire Island was also significant, with average profile volume loss and overwash volumes that were nearly the same as those for eastern Fire Island. In addition, distinct differences in the characteristics of the overwash deposits on eastern Fire Island, as opposed to western Fire Island, appear related to pre-existing differences in island width and elevation. To the west, the deposits were more sheet-like and did not penetrate as far inland as the overwash fans and surge channels to the east. Central Fire Island had relatively little overwash, which was primarily focused in areas with pre-existing cuts or lows in the dunes. Beaches and dunes in the central region were heavily eroded and narrowed, but infrequent overwash and relatively little U_b migration result in the lowest average profile volume loss (11 percent less than for eastern and western Fire Island).

Field data collection of cross-shore profiles and along-shore metrics (shoreline, upper beach) continued monthly through April 2013. Following Sandy, frequent winter storms led to ongoing erosion and volume loss from November 2012 to March 2013. Based on field profiles, western Fire Island had higher overall rates of erosion and greater post-winter recovery (for example, more active profile) than central Fire Island. Beach widening and profile elevation gains observed during the last survey (April 9, 2013) indicate that sand is being returned to the beach from offshore. Profile volume increased on average by 18.9 percent; however, recent recovery has restored only a fraction of the original (pre-Sandy) volumes to the beaches at Fire Island. At the end of the 6-month post-Sandy survey period, the volume of the beach remains 40 percent less than the pre-Sandy condition.

References

Hapke, C.J., Lentz, E.E., Gayes, P.T., McCoy, C.A., Hehre, R.E., Schwab, W.C., and Williams, S.J., 2010, A review of sediment budget imbalances along Fire Island, New York—Can nearshore geologic framework and patterns of shoreline change explain the deficit?: Journal of Coastal Research, v. 26, p. 510–522.

Kratzmann, M.G., and Hapke, C., 2012, Quantifying anthropogenically driven morphologic changes on a barrier island—Fire Island National Seashore, New York: Journal of Coastal Research, v. 28, p. 76–88.

Leatherman, S.P., and Allen, J.R., 1985, Geomorphic Analysis, Fire Island Inlet to Montauk Point, Long Island, New York, Reformulation Study. National Park Service for the U.S. Army Corps of Engineers.

Lentz, E.E., and Hapke, C., 2011, Geologic framework influences on the geomorphology of an anthropogenically modified barrier island—Assessment of dune/beach changes at Fire Island, New York: Geomorphology, v. 126, p. 82–96.

Lentz, E.E., Hapke, C.J., Stockdon, H.F., and Hehre, R.E., 2013, Improving understanding of near-term barrier island evolution through multi-decadal assessment of morphologic change: Marine Geology, v. 337, p. 125–139.

National Oceanic and Atmospheric Administration, Ocean Service, National Geodetic Survey, 2013, Hurricane SANDY: Rapid Response Imagery Viewer, accessed August 7, 2013, at *http://ngs.woc.noaa.gov/storms/sandy/*.

Schwab, W.C., Baldwin, W.E., Hapke, C.J., Lentz, E.E., Gayes, P.T., Denny, J.F., List, J.H., and Warner, J.C., 2013, Geologic evidence for onshore sediment transport from the Inner Continental Shelf—Fire Island, New York: Journal of Coastal Research, v. 29, no. 3, p. 526–544.

Stockdon, H.F., Doran, K.J., Sopkin, K.L., Smith, K.E.L., and Fredericks, Xan, 2013, Coastal topography–Northeast Atlantic coast, post-Hurricane Sandy, 2012: U.S. Geological Survey Data Series 765.

Thieler, E.R., Himmelstoss, E.A., Zichichi, J.L., and Ergul, A., 2009, Digital Shoreline Analysis System (DSAS) version 4.0 — An ArcGIS extension for calculating shoreline change: U.S. Geological Survey Open-File Report 2008-1278.

Weber, K.M., List, J.H., and Morgan, K.M., 2005, An operational mean high water datum for determination of shoreline position from topographic lidar data: U.S. Geological Survey Open-File Report 2005-1027, available at *http://pubs.usgs.gov/of/2005/1027/index.html*.

Appendix 1

Cross-shore elevation profiles (upper panel) and associated profile volume in m^3/m (lower panel) collected during nine field surveys (October 28, 2012 to April 9, 2013) at nine DGPS profile locations along Fire Island, New York, are contained in Appendix 1.

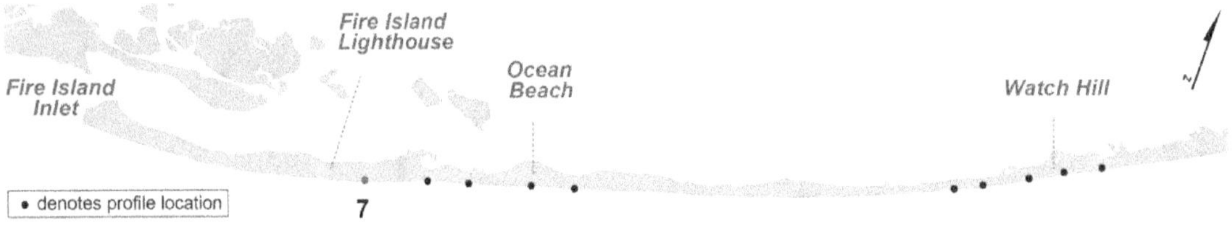

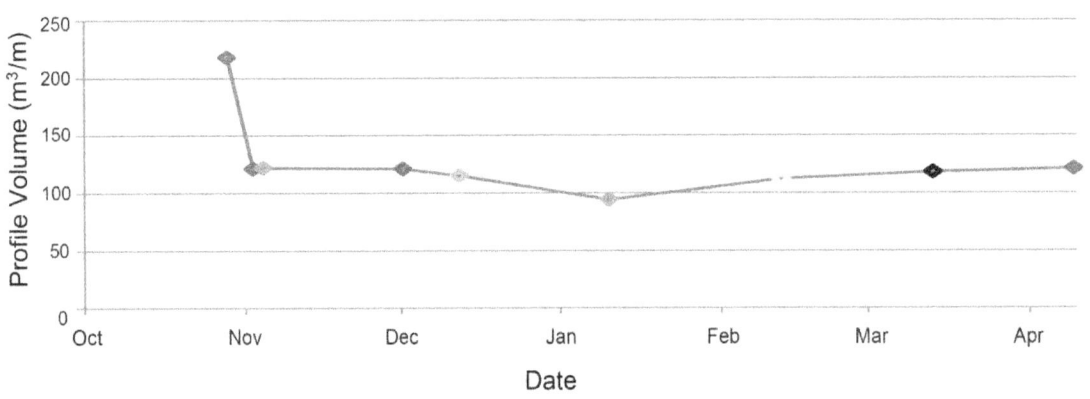

Profile 7

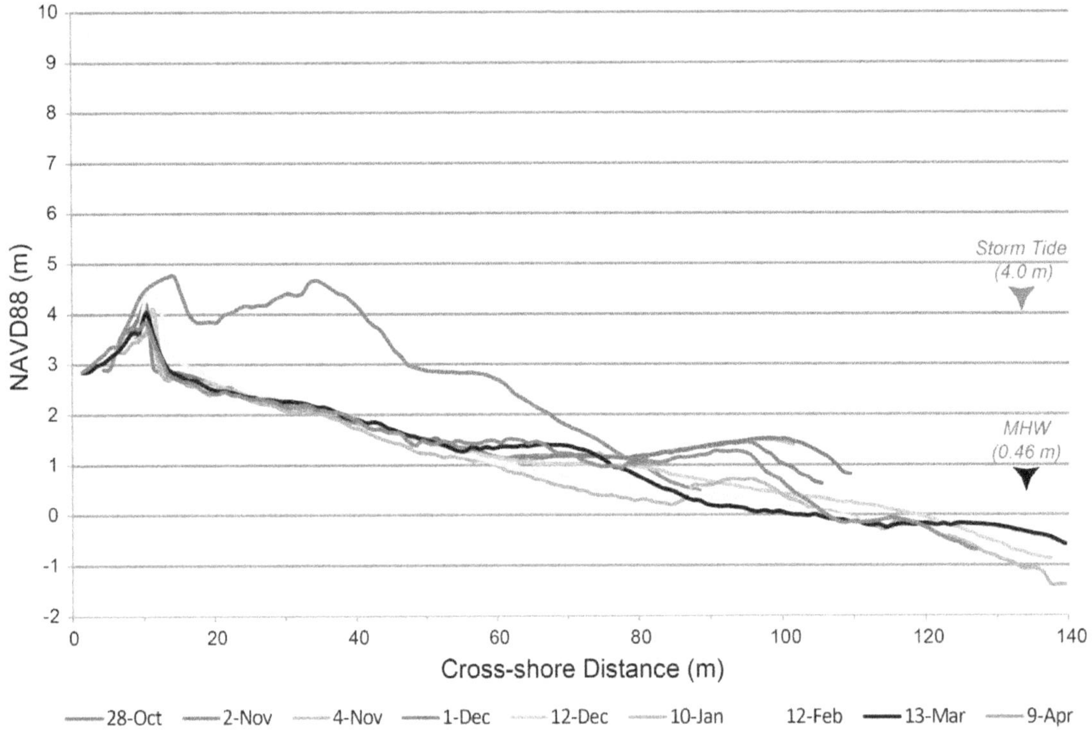

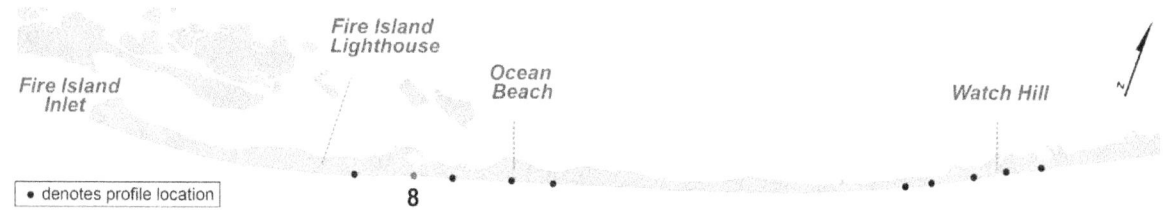

Profile 8

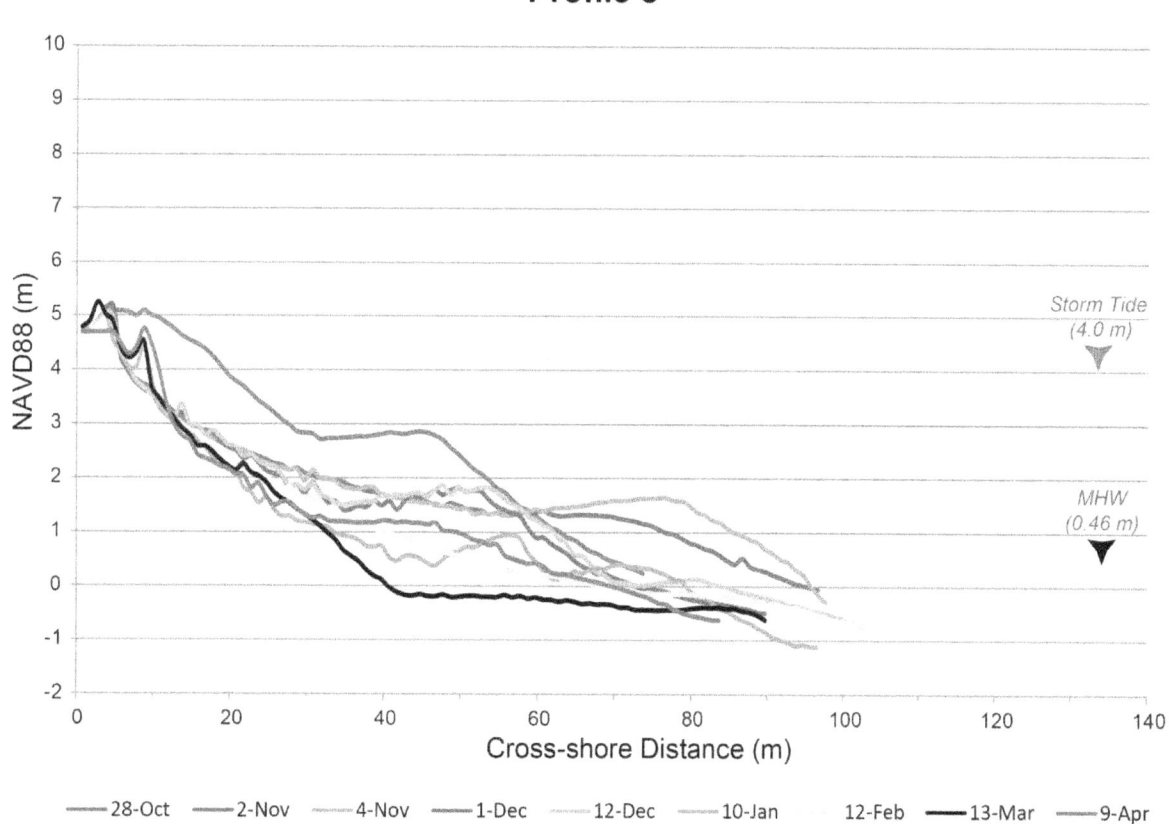

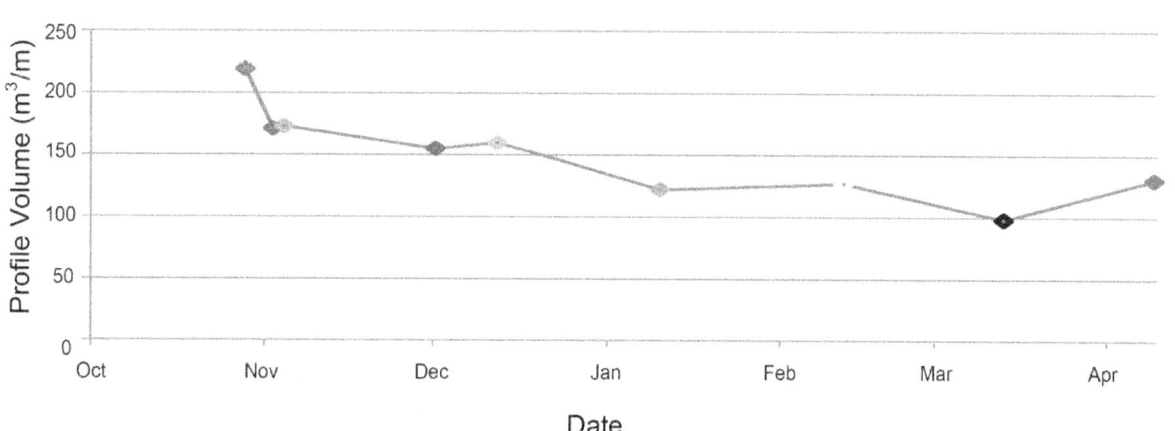

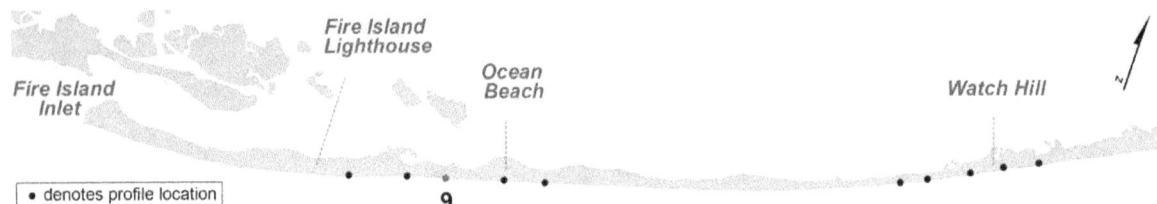

Profile 9

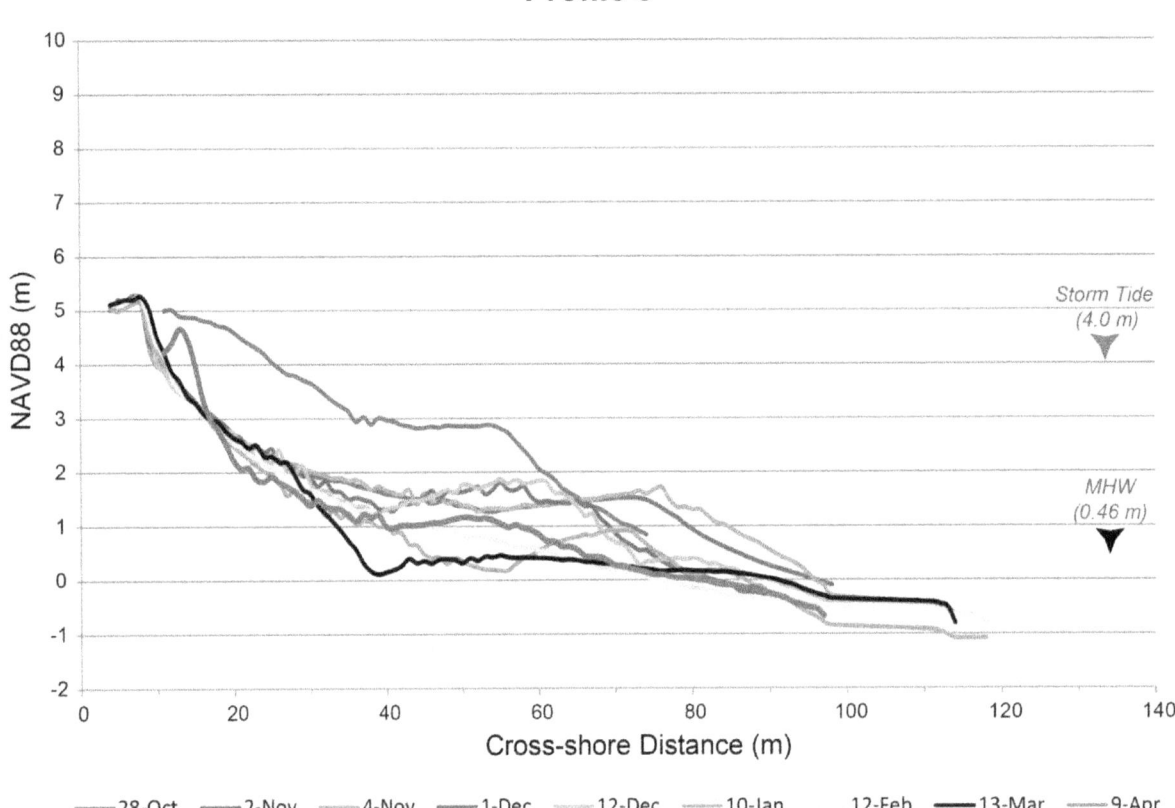

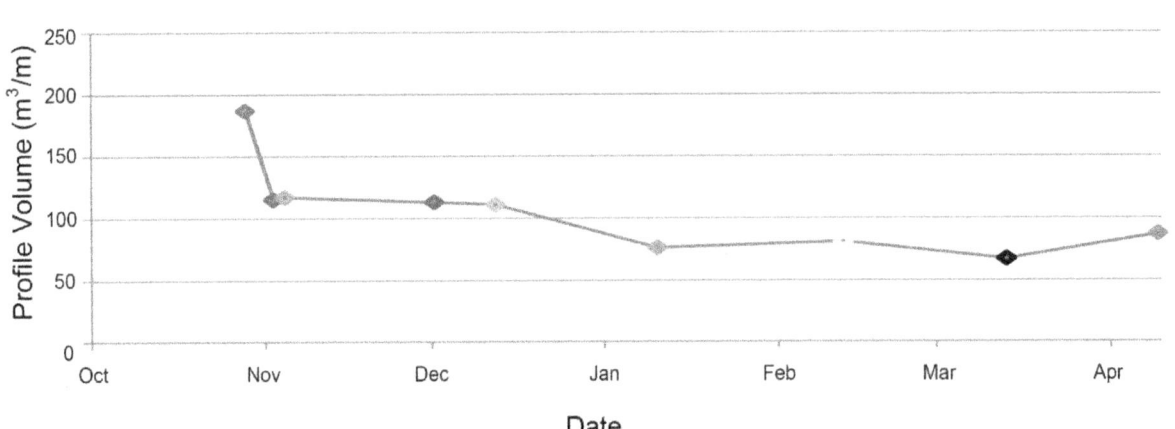

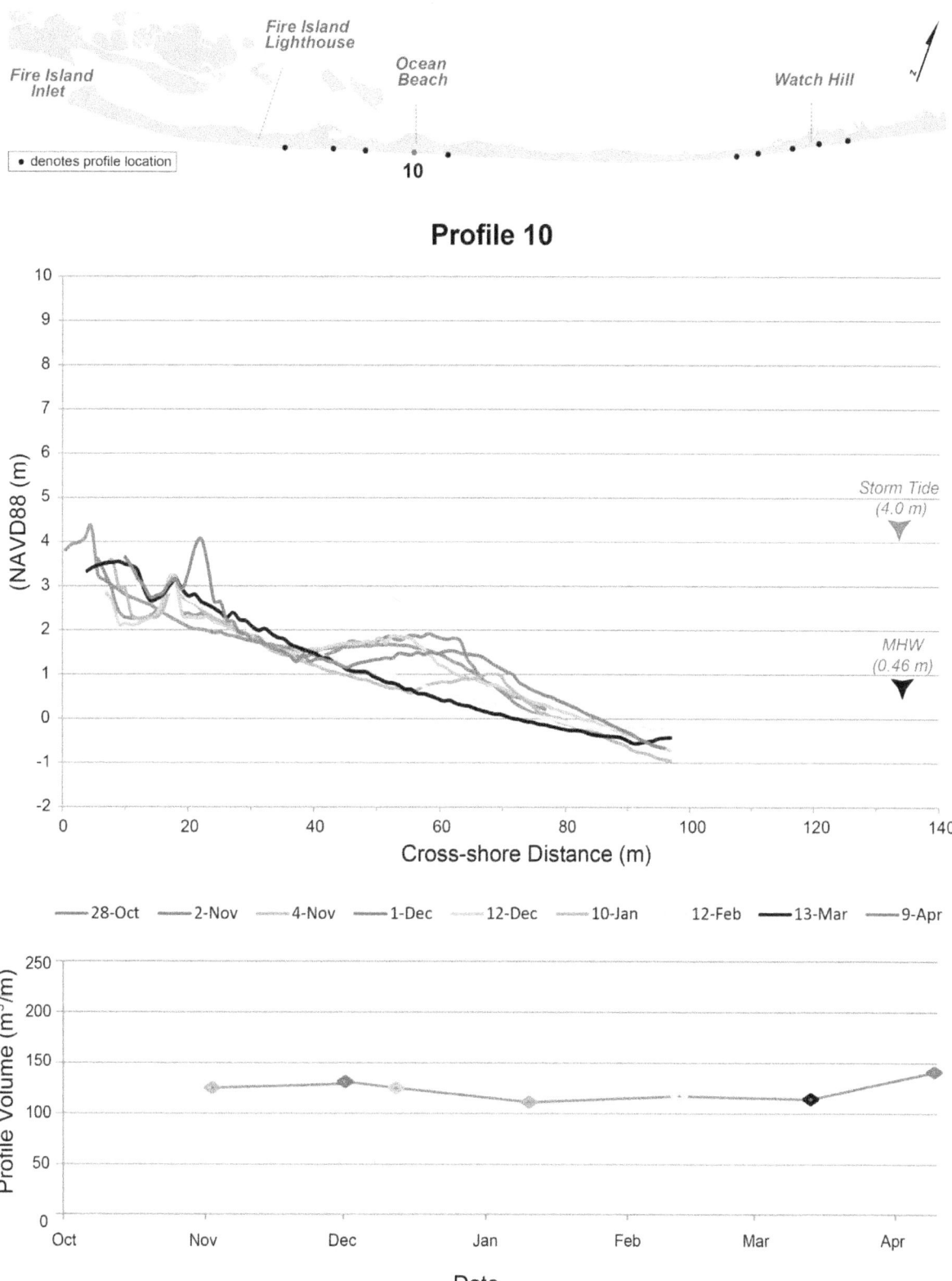

Profile 10

Cross-shore Distance (m)

(NAVD88 (m))

Storm Tide
(4.0 m)

MHW
(0.46 m)

28-Oct · 2-Nov · 4-Nov · 1-Dec · 12-Dec · 10-Jan · 12-Feb · 13-Mar · 9-Apr

Profile Volume (m³/m)

Date

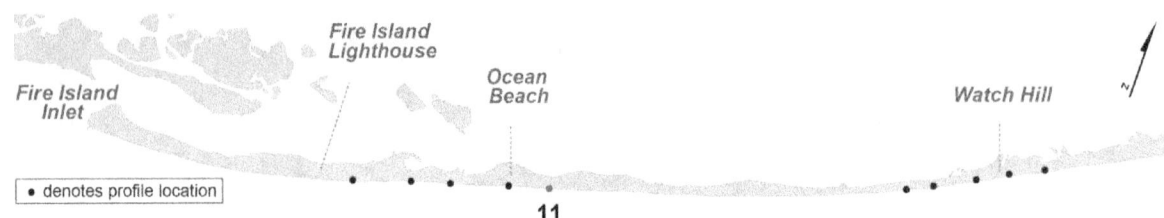

Profile 11

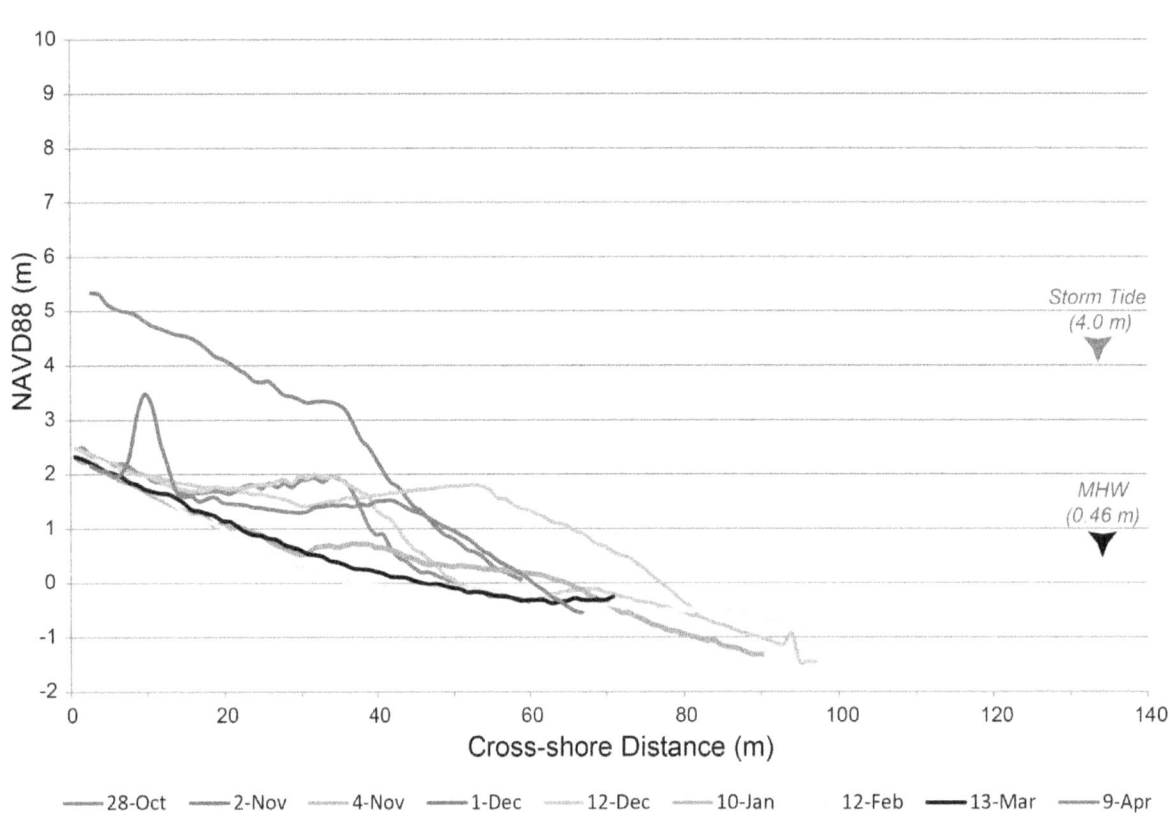

28-Oct ——— 2-Nov ——— 4-Nov ——— 1-Dec ——— 12-Dec ——— 10-Jan ——— 12-Feb ——— 13-Mar ——— 9-Apr

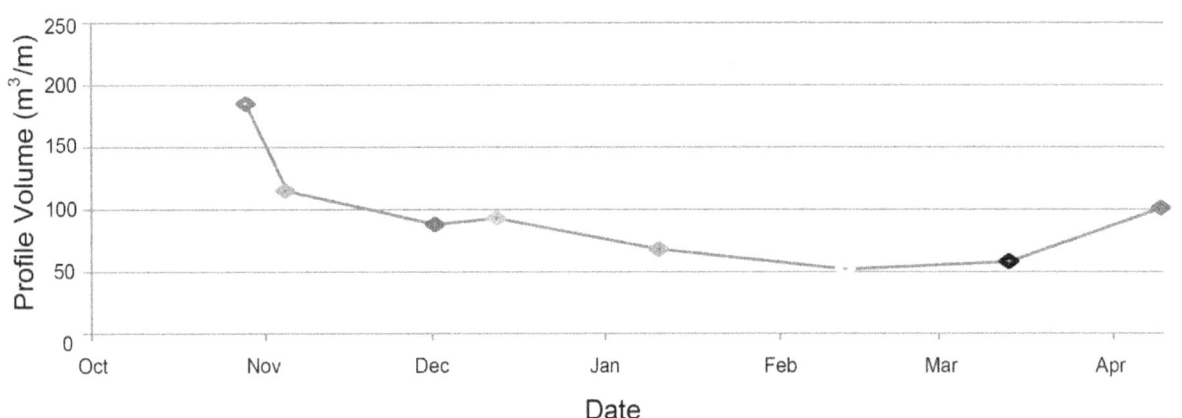

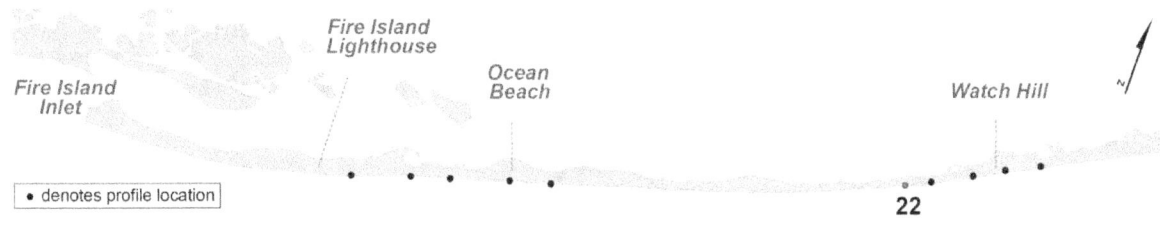

Profile 22

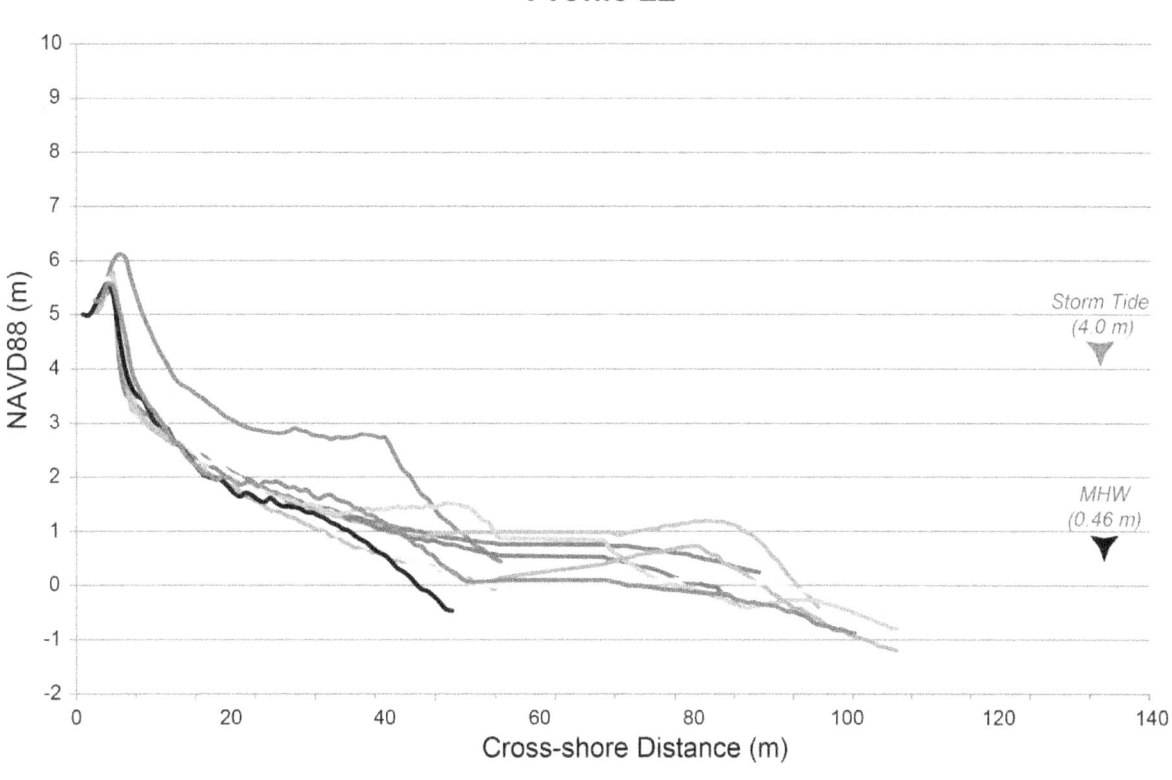

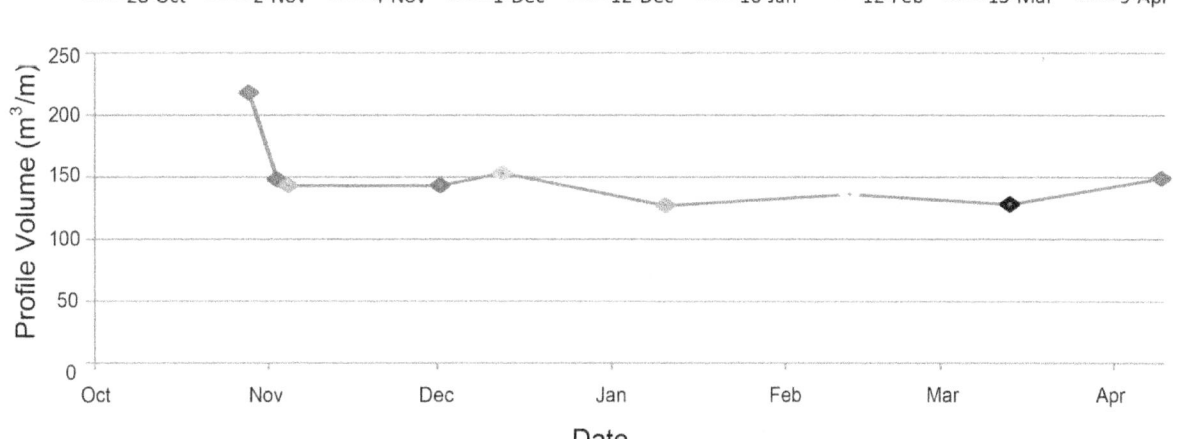

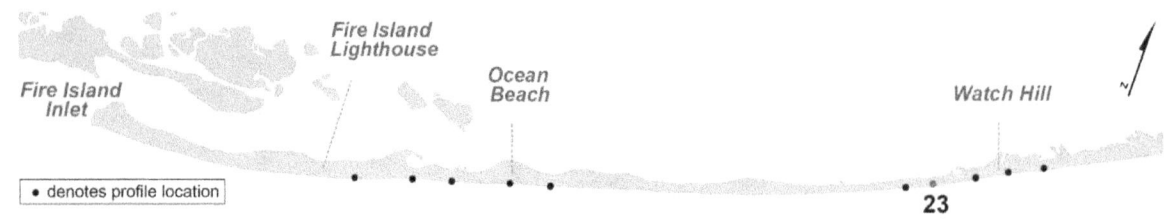

Profile 23

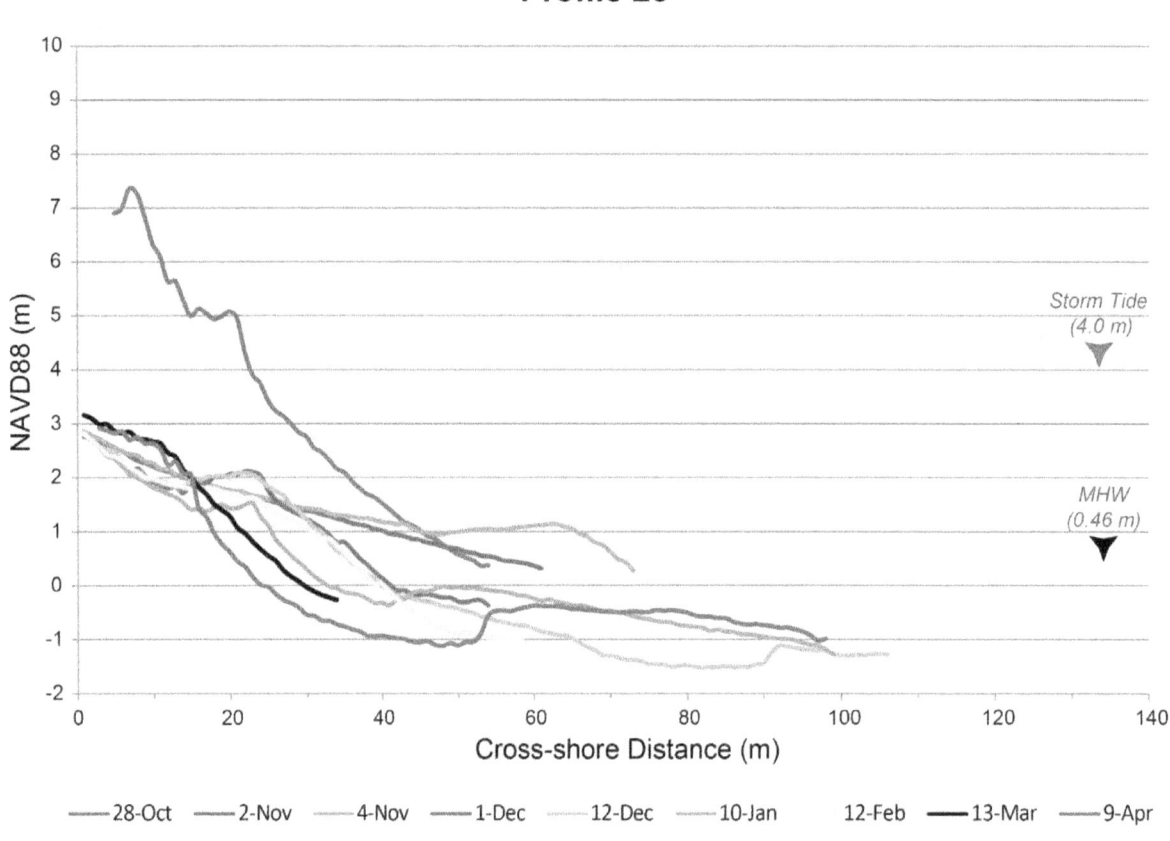

Legend: 28-Oct — 2-Nov — 4-Nov — 1-Dec — 12-Dec — 10-Jan — 12-Feb — 13-Mar — 9-Apr

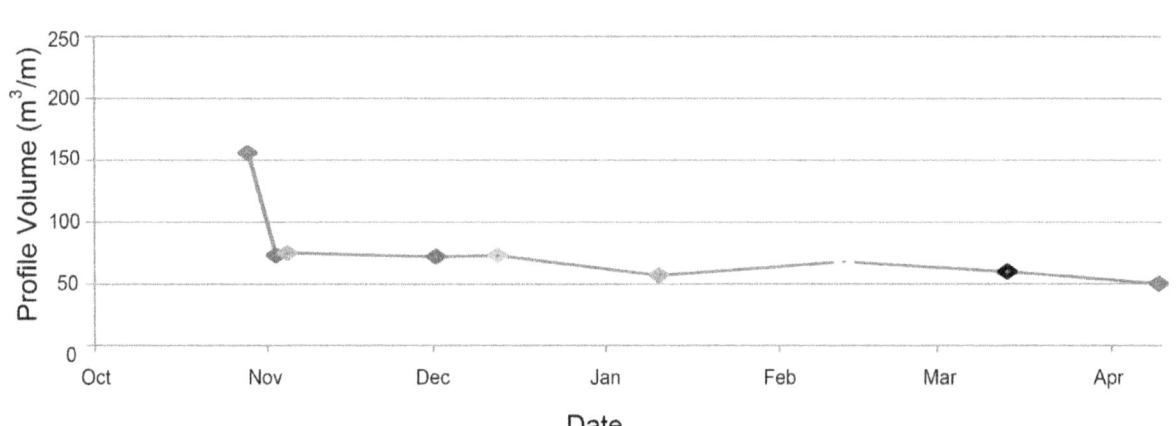

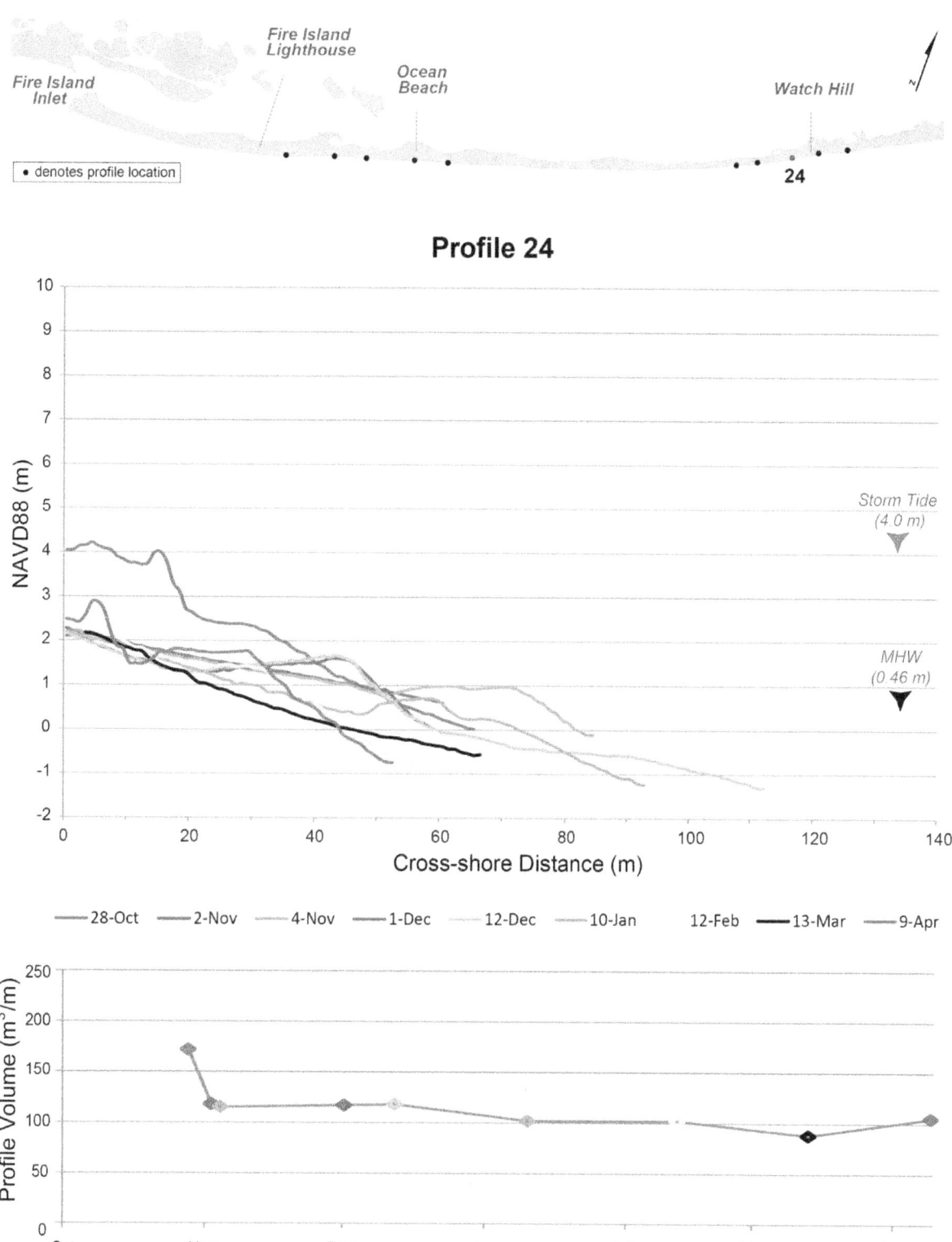

Profile 24

Legend: 28-Oct, 2-Nov, 4-Nov, 1-Dec, 12-Dec, 10-Jan, 12-Feb, 13-Mar, 9-Apr

Fire Island Lighthouse
Fire Island Inlet
Ocean Beach
Watch Hill
25
• denotes profile location

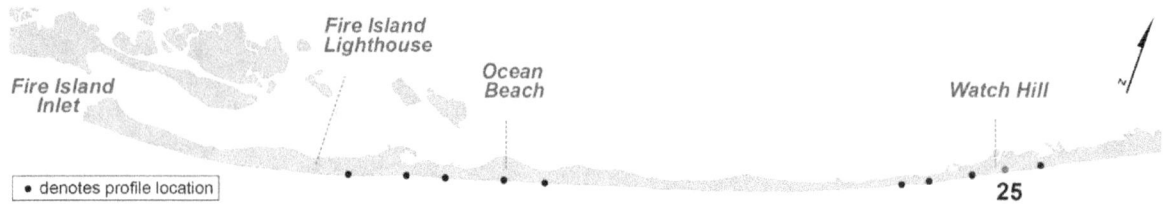

Profile 25
NAVD88 (m)
Cross-shore Distance (m)
Storm Tide (4.0 m)
MHW (0.46 m)
28-Oct
2-Nov
4-Nov
1-Dec
12-Dec
10-Jan
12-Feb
13-Mar
9-Apr

Profile Volume (m³/m)
Date
Oct
Nov
Dec
Jan
Feb
Mar
Apr

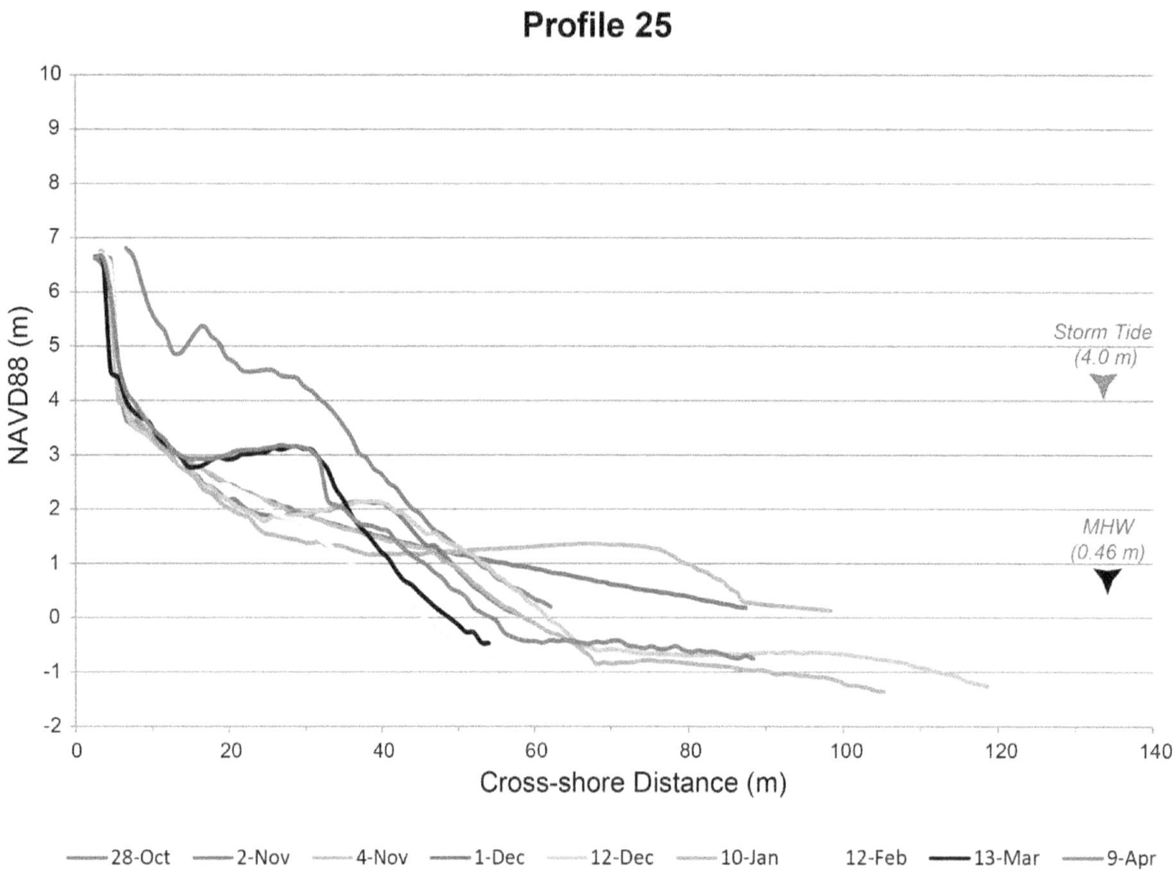

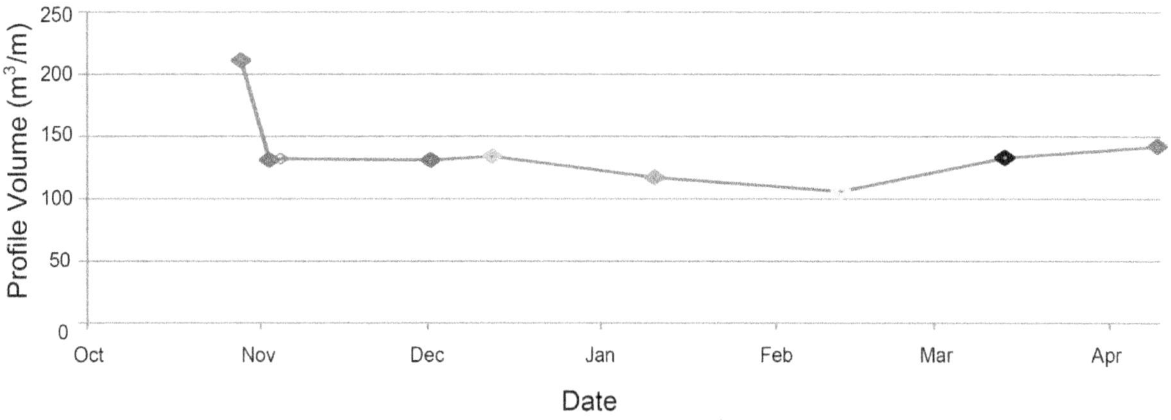

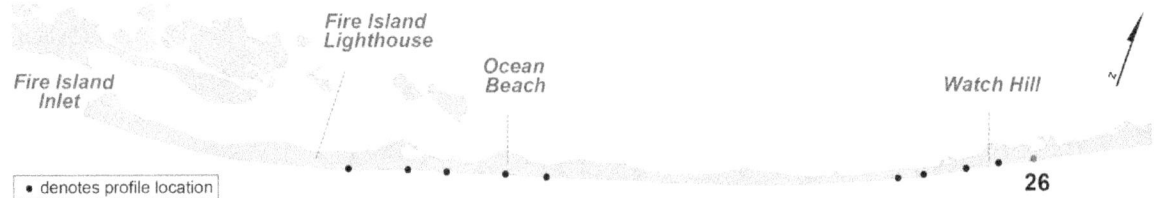

Fire Island Inlet
Fire Island Lighthouse
Ocean Beach
Watch Hill
N
• denotes profile location
26

Profile 26

NAVD88 (m)
Storm Tide (4.0 m)
MHW (0.46 m)
Cross-shore Distance (m)
28-Oct
2-Nov
4-Nov
1-Dec
12-Dec
10-Jan
12-Feb
13-Mar
9-Apr

Profile Volume (m^3/m)
Oct
Nov
Dec
Jan
Feb
Mar
Apr
Date

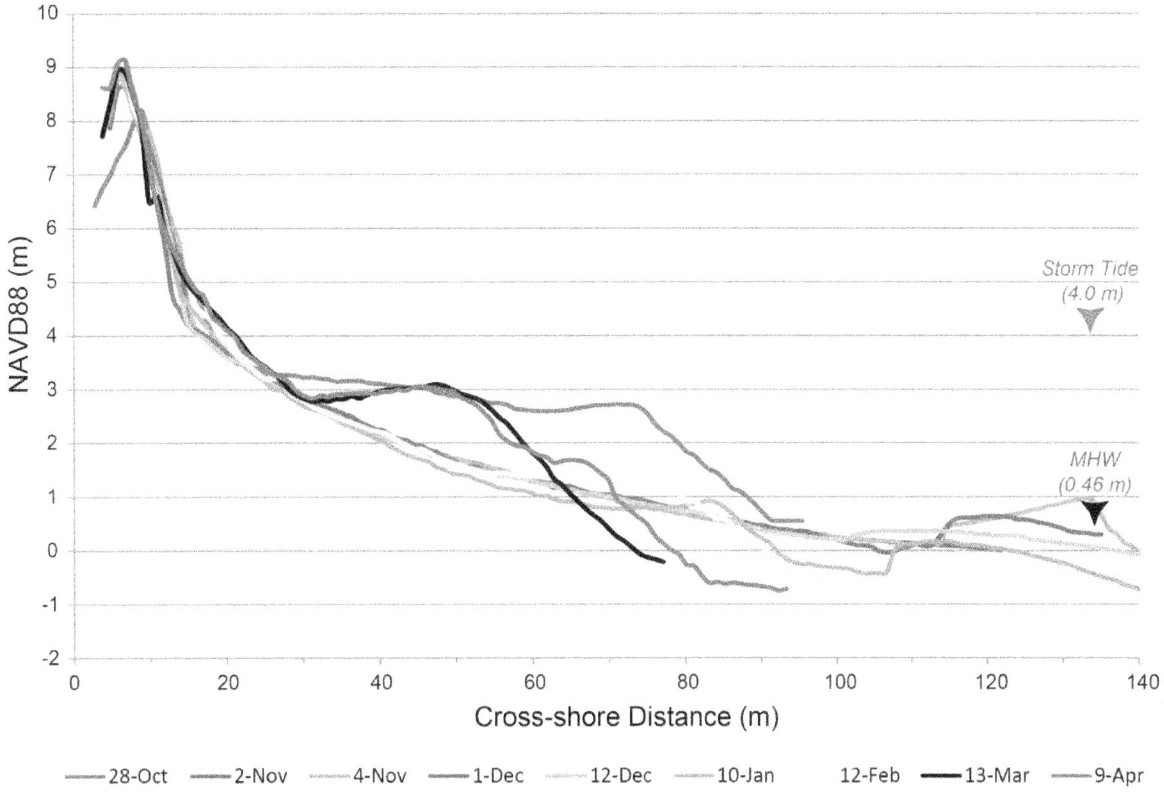

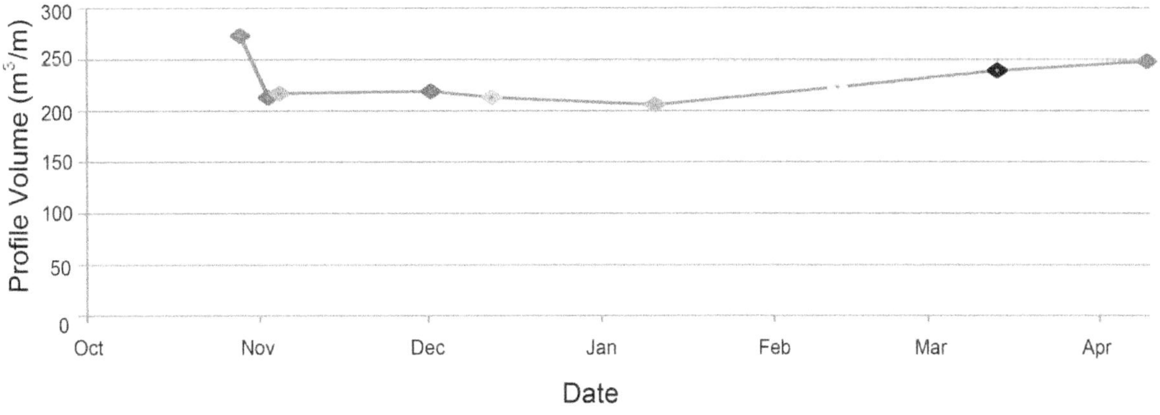